GOD'S PURPOSE AND PLAN FOR YOUR LIFE

Non-Denominational Sermons

By: Grant Harrison

Edited by: Christa and Andre Savage

Trilogy Christian Publishers
A Wholly Owned Subsidiary of Trinity Broadcasting Network
2442 Michelle Drive
Tustin, CA 92780
Gods Purpose and Plan for Your Life
Nondenominational Sermons
Copyright © 2021 by Grant Harrison
All Scripture quotations, unless otherwise noted, taken from THE HOLY BIBLE, KING JAMES VERSION®, KJV® Copyright © 1973, 1978, 1984, 2011 by Biblica, Inc.® Used by permission. All rights reserved worldwide.
Scripture quotations marked (KJV) taken from The Holy Bible, King James Version. Cambridge Edition: 1769.
All rights reserved, including the right to reproduce this book or portions thereof in any form whatsoever.
For information, address Trilogy Christian Publishing
Rights Department, 2442 Michelle Drive, Tustin, Ca 92780.
Trilogy Christian Publishing/ TBN and colophon are trademarks of Trinity Broadcasting Network.
For information about special discounts for bulk purchases, please contact Trilogy Christian Publishing.
Manufactured in the United States of America

These sermons may be available as an audio product. Visit: http://www.gmcdelectronicpublishing.com for more information. Many of the scriptures cited within this book are identified within Appendix A.

10 9 8 7 6 5 4 3 2 1
Library of Congress Cataloging-in-Publication Data is available.
ISBN 978-1-64773-937-9
ISBN 978-1-64773-938-6 (ebook)

God's Purpose and Plan for your Life

We are all at different stages on our Christian walk with the Lord, and we want to partner with you in this latest stage of your Christian adventure! Please send to the addresses below your comments about this book and how it has prepared you for the next stage in your life. Thank you.

Artwork by G E Harrison, Copyright © 2021 Grant Harrison. Printed in the United States of America.

Scripture quotations marked as KJV are taken from the King James Version of the Bible, copyright © 1611

Table of Contents

TABLE OF CONTENTS

Acknowledgements...V

Foreword..VII

Introduction..IX

Sermon 1– In the Midst...............................11

Sermon 2– Rock of My Salvation....................31

Sermon 3– His Path to our Spiritual Recovery...55

Sermon 4– The Holy Spirit in Us....................79

Sermon 5– Jesus, Our Lord, Makes Us New All Over...105

Sermon 6– Loving.......................................127

Sermon 7– Partners....................................141

Appendix A– Sermon Scripture References....173

Additional Resources..................................175

Additional Online Resources.......................177

ACKNOWLEDGMENTS

First, giving thanks to Our Heavenly Father, Our Savior Jesus Christ, and the Blessed Holy Spirit, through whom I was guided and inspired to write this book. Also, heartfelt thanks to all those men of God who have influenced the many lessons learned from the Holy Scriptures, across several Christian ministries, and through several churches, most notably, Tree of Life Bible Church, of Centreville, Virginia!

My sincerest thanks and gratitude goes out to pastors such as James A. Vanison Sr. and Leon Jackson, as well as elders such as Rob Hunter, deacons such as the late Robert Hickman, and the closest of Christian friends, all of whom have impacted me along God's Path and Purpose for my life and the development of this book.

Next, I want to personally thank Christa and Andre Savage for dedicating the time and effort to tirelessly edit this book, and without whom, this book never would have been realized! Additional thanks go out to Leonard Jackson and Latoya Hunter for making my original sermon recording. For any others who inspired the development of this work, but whom I have forgotten to mention, God bless you all!

FOREWORD

The Bible tells us God sends to the church such as are needed. God sent me a beloved and effective "son in the ministry," named Grant Harrison. He graduated from the University of Pittsburgh in 1989 and American University in 1999. During this time, Grant started attending Tree of Life Bible Church of Centreville, VA, in 1989, and through his service, has been elevated to deacon, minister, and assistant pastor. Along with regularly leading morning services and mid-week Bible Study teachings at our church, he has preached in many churches throughout Virginia, Maryland, and Pennsylvania.

As God's servant, Grant participated in various mission trips to places including Ghana, West Africa, Uganda, East Africa, Jamaica, West Indies, and Guatemala, Central America to preach God's Word and teach God's Purpose. He has an undying belief in the power of prayer in Christ Jesus, as well as the completeness of Almighty God in miraculously providing and protecting us all. He lives a fear-free life in the Holy Spirit by living his favorite scripture "God did not give us the spirit of fear, but of power, and of love, and of a sound mind!"

James A. Vanison, Sr.
The founding Pastor of Tree of Life Bible Church of Centreville, Virginia

INTRODUCTION

This book is for those Christians who want to serve the Lord in new and more profound ways. If you have already received your calling and are a new minister of God, this book may help you develop new sermons of your own as the Holy Spirit leads you. On the other hand, if you have been faithfully serving God's people, then you too are a minister of the Gospel of Jesus Christ because the word "minister" means "servant." This book helps you study God's Word through sermon messages, online pastoral resources, and other encouragements along the way.

Throughout the writing of this book, I prayerfully prepared each sermon after being first led by God. I pray that these sermons help develop your walk with the Lord, and help your preaching and teaching of His people, all the while opening your spiritual eyes to all that God has in store for you and the ministry He has placed within you.

This book is unique because it is most notably a word-by-word transcription of s sermons preached over the pulpits of various churches in Virginia, Maryland, and Pennsylvania. You will notice subtle references or sayings based upon how I speak and preach. The point here is that you and your personality will come out in your preaching as well, and that is good. because God doesn't want you to be another T. D.

Introduction

Jakes, Joel Osteen, or even Billy Graham. Instead, He wants you to be the best version of you!

Many of the scripture references used within each sermon are in the appendix. Additional Biblical resources are also included in an appendix in this book.

May God richly bless you and your family as you learn God's Purpose and Plan for your life and as you serve and protect God's people and not hurt or abuse them!

An associated website has other resources and audio versions of each sermon.

Sermon 1 – In the Midst

Verses: 2 Thessalonians 1:1-12
(Originally preached on May 25, 2003)

"So that we ourselves glory in you in the churches of God for your patience and faith in all your persecutions and tribulations that ye endure: Which is a manifest token of the righteous judgment of God, that ye may be counted worthy of the kingdom of God, for which ye also suffer."

2 Thessalonians 1:4-5, KJV

First, giving honor to God for blessing me through all these years and for calling me to come and speak to you tonight, I give Him all honor and praise. I guess if I had to think of what I'm thankful most about right now tonight, I would say I thank Him for being Truth. He can be described as Truth as an adjective, but He is Truth. There is no variableness in Him. He doesn't have the potential to lie. He is Truth, and I thank God for that.

That means that all the things that we believe of Him are true, right? Because you wouldn't want to spend your whole life believing in Him and there be even one aspect of Him

Sermon 1 – In the Midst

that's not true. What if when you die, and you get to heaven, He says, "Remember when I said I'll let you live for eternity? That wasn't true. It was partially true, maybe somewhat true. You live maybe 1,000 years, but then that's it."

We will live for eternity. Why? Because He said so, amen? I thank God because He is inspiring. He made us alive. I don't mean in the physical because when He made you alive the first time, you didn't even know who you were. You were a baby. I'm talking about when He inspired you the second time to be reborn, amen? To be born again spiritually is an aspect of your being alive as it hadn't been prior, and I thank God for that. Do you know why? Because no one else could have done it. I thank God for being an on-time God.

I sat up here and listened to all the testimonies, and you get excited hearing how good God has been to everyone, but I'm going to tell you something. I think each one of us has a dynamic testimony, but sometimes, it's just like one of the ministers said earlier, "we come in carrying our load." And hopefully, God willing, when you leave up out of here, after hearing this Word that God has presented for you, you won't leave with that same load carried behind you. So, I thank God for that.

My Recent Testimony

I'm going to give my testimony if you don't mind. I was coming back from my vacation, and as I was driving up the road, I noticed someone ghosting me. I don't know if you recognize this type of driving on the highway, but there is a technique some people do, and I call it "ghosting you." That is, whenever they come up from behind you, and they stay in your blind spot and slightly behind you for miles and miles. I don't really like that because they should change lanes or do something else because if I have to hit the brakes fast or swerve, they will hit me from behind.

On this particular day, a woman was doing this, and the Holy Spirit said to me it is time to let this woman pass me. I used the opportunity to go ahead and pull over and get some gas for my car and a bottle of water for myself. When I got back on the road, it was no more than about ten minutes later when there was a huge tractor-trailer in front of me and even more cars ahead of the tractor-trailer all stuck in traffic. It was that kind of traffic where you are not going anywhere. It was like a parking lot, and people were getting out of their cars and looking up the street to see what was going on.

I couldn't see what was up the road, but I saw this plume of black smoke. This was in the twilight of the night, so that should show you how contrasting it was. It turns out that a tractor-trailer had done something and gone off the road and exploded because of the gas tanks it was carrying. I was praying all the way that the driver was fine. And I don't know what happens to that woman in the car that was ghosting me throughout all of this. But who is to say that wasn't my time?

I could have ignored the unction of the Holy Spirit and been killed as part of that accident. I could have died all because I had not yielded to the Holy Spirit. Instead, I was safe, but it could have been the other way, and I thank God!

That's what we have been hearing in testimonies all tonight about yielding to the Spirit. When the spirit says pull over, PULL OVER. Don't push your way to get a car that God doesn't want you to have or to get a house that He does not want you to have or to get that man or that woman that He does not want you to have. Thank God for Him being Almighty.

Giving Thanks to God and Pastor

I want to thank God for my pastor. I was reading our daily scriptures, and it said in Jeremiah 3:15, "And I will give you pastors according to my heart." That means that our pastor was chosen to come here. There are churches in northern VA that do not have a pastor, but your pastor is sitting right over there. It also says, "and he shall feed you with knowledge and understanding." Now, who does that sound like? Surely, that sounds like our pastor! So, I want to give honor where honor is due. Pastor, I want to thank you for being our pastor for all these years.

I also want to thank you for sharing your pulpit. There are a lot of pastors that will not share their pulpit. I thank God for my pastor, and I thank God for all of you for coming out on a

God's Purpose and Plan for your Life

holiday Sunday night. I also want to add a special thank you to our awesome choir. Their singing, praise, and worship have blown me away.

Now, let's get into God's Word. The topic tonight is going to be "in the midst." You are going to laugh and chuckle about how much this sermon is tangled up in what you have been testifying about. It's like God is confirming all of your testimonies, and that's why I'm sitting up here getting so happy. Pastor said that when God plants a message in you, it's like you are pregnant. All that spiritual pressure of God's message within you builds up and grows until you don't feel right again until you have birthed that message out to His people. So, let me go ahead and birth this message. The scripture I'm coming from is 2 Thessalonians 1:1-12, and this is all tangled up in pastor's message from this morning.

I always start off with a question. Why is there suffering in the world? Or put another more personal way, if I'm already saved, why do I have to suffer? We may not admit to it, but sometimes we feel this way. Why am I not getting the promotions I think I should get, and why am I not moving along economically like I see my neighbors are when they might not even be saved. There are reasons for these things. Why am I having health problems? There is a reason for it, amen? This is exciting for me on a bunch of different levels. I'm going to start back in the beginning just to give you some insight into what's going on in the background, so let me tell you about the

Sermon 1 – In the Midst

second letter of Paul.

Apparently, there were problems in Thessalonica, and they centered around that Paul had gained a lot of Christian zeal and excitement, but the people there weren't as rooted and grounded in the Word of God as they should have been. When you're not rooted and grounded in God's Word, what can happen is you can go off on a tangent, and you don't have the Word of God to hold on to. So, what had happened was someone there in Thessalonica had started a rumor that Christ had already died, rose again, and returned. Then, they started thinking He will be back any day now. Soon, they were quitting their jobs and selling all that they had, assuming that they didn't need it and they were just going to wait. When Paul got word of this because you know back in that day, word spread from mouth to mouth and got around just like today, and so he had to straighten them out. So, Paul sent them this second letter. He sets up the letter in two parts. He started off with "here is what you're not understanding," and "this is the punishment that is going to come to those playing around with the Holy Spirit." What does that mean to us in 2003? It means that we need to get ourselves right with God. or God's punishment will surely come.

If you look at the first two verses, it starts with "grace," which is a Greek greeting, and "peace," which is a Hebrew greeting. This is an introduction of who Paul is and who he represented, and Paul and the Christians were well known.

Verse 2 reads, "We ought always to thank God for you, brothers and sisters, and rightly so, because your faith is growing more and more, and the love all of you have for one another is increasing." The importance of this verse is that you must understand that, during this time, the church was in tribulation.

In the first book of Thessalonians, he praised them for doing a good job. But he must come back and tell them that they are still doing good in that area and the importance of continuing to do good that they are doing while in the midst of their tribulations. What sets us apart today is that we know Christ's life, death, burial, and resurrection, amen. That's what keeps us grounded in our decisions here at this church. We know that Christ sits on the right hand of the Father.

When I spoke last Sunday, the Lord laid it on my heart to talk about "the Seed." The Seed was prophesied way back in Genesis 3:15. It described how God's official Seed would travel down through the lines and be manifested in Christ.

Jesus is the Seed

Later on, in the Bible, Jesus gives us a parable of the Seed and how it can lay on the pathway where it is tamped down and not really cultivated per se. Some Seed that lands there, the birds would come eat it up. Later on, He also talks about if the Seed fell on stony ground or it lands among thorns rather than good soil. The Seed is Jesus, and the good cultivat-

Sermon 1 – In the Midst

ed ground or the tamped down pathway, with thorns or with stones, not only represent four different types of Christians, but they also represent four different types of stages of our Christian walk within all of us.

There were times when our heart was just as hard as that path. The word was preached to us, and we didn't take it seriously. The message wasn't real to us; it didn't sink down. Then there were times when the Seed was planted in the stony ground, and it did sprout, but it didn't take root, and because it didn't root, whenever the sun came, it died and was no more. It talks about that same situation when the Seed fell on a heart that was stony in that this person hears the Word but doesn't truly accept the Word, and as a result, that little which he had was stolen away. God forbid that there were times in our life when the Seed fell among thorns, where we believed, and we received, but we were so tangled up in the cares of this world like the guy that is sitting on the fence. He wants to be in the club and in the church. That is a carnal Christian. It's not that you're not a Christian...instead, it's just that you haven't completely come out of the world.

No one can judge another because we were all that way, and we have all been at various stages in our walk with Christ. But, praise God for the good cultivated ground. This is that one time when perhaps we were out in the world, and the Good Gospel message was preached to us, or someone testified to us, and we sincerely accepted God's forgiveness for

God's Purpose and Plan for your Life

our sin and asked Jesus to come into our heart! And, immediately, things are starting to get more peaceful. Soon after, we started to realize just why God allowed us to go through certain things in our lives and why God allowed us to experience certain trials.

When the Seed finally gets firmly planted in your heart, **it must grow**.

When the Seed finally gets firmly planted in your heart, it must grow. When the Seed finally gets firmly planted in your heart, it must grow. If it doesn't grow, then fruit isn't borne, and then there must not be Seed in there. The Seed needs good cultivated soil on your pathway of life. There is something in that soil that will make it grow because soil is made up of dirt filled with nitrogen and the other various nutrients that the Seeds need to burst through its shell and grow.

God desires to prepare (and cultivate) every heart if you will allow Him to do so. All of us need to look at our life with Christ and analyze, are we giving all of ourselves to Him? If you want to go through stage one (tamped pathways and birds) and then through stage two (stony ground), and then through stage three (thorny ground), go ahead.But if you are smart and you want to go straight to stage four (good cultivated ground), then let God have that good ground of your heart dug up and cultivated with some good fertilizer in there. He Him-

Sermon 1 – In the Midst

self will put that Seed down deep in your heart and will water it, that it will grow. He Himself will put that Seed down deep in your heart and will water it, that it will grow.

> He Himself will put that Seed down deep in your heart and will water it, that **it will grow.**

There is a warning in there, and that comes from another parable Jesus taught us. He warns, "If branches don't bear fruit, they will be cast down, thrown into the fire, and burned!" We don't want any of that for any of us, do we? Touch your neighbor and tell them, "Don't get burned up!"

In verse 3 of 2 Thessalonians, again it says, "In the midst of their trials their faith grew, and the love all of you have for one another is increasing." That is a sign of growth in you. Who can tell me what the Seed is? The Seed is the Word of God. What is the Word of God? Jesus is the Word of God. So, when you say I have Jesus way down deep on the inside, then you've got God's Word way down deep on the inside. What you want to do is to get Jesus way down deep inside you. It's not that the works you do save you because salvation is a free gift from God to you, but once you are saved, you will do works.

In verse 4, Paul was exceedingly excited about this church because it had become a model church. During their trials, they were rejoicing. Some people have gotten up and testified about the problems they are having, but the importance is to bless the Lord in spite of our trials and tribulations and that we keep a close relationship with God in the midst of our trials and tribulations. In the midst of our trials, keep God in the midst; in this very trial you are dealing with today and that you came into church with today. You have to know that while you're going through your tribulation, whose eyes are on you. It is the eyes of the people of this world, on your job, your neighbors, your closest friends, and even your family.

Maybe God has been blessing you, and you haven't had many tribulations because I don't hear enough amens. But, let me tell you something that is a guarantee. Trials will come. If you are not going through something right now, it is coming. And, when it does, there is a right way to succeed in it and a wrong way to fail in it. So, this ministry of prevention is giving you all the right answers. Number 1, you want to love one another in the midst of your trials, and you want to have Christ in the midst of your tribulations, amen?

In verse 5, which is a manifest token of the righteous judgment of God? It is "that ye may be counted worthy of the kingdom of God, for which ye also suffer." So, here we are suffering for the kingdom of God, and that proves that God is the author and finisher of our faith. So, the question is why are we joyful in tribulation, and the answer is because God is still in control. It is He that works within our trials. It's not

Sermon 1 – In the Midst

that God gives us trials because God never tempted anyone. But, through the works of the devil and through sometimes the lust of our own mind, we have a tendency to get ourselves in trouble.

In the midst of that trial and tribulation, we must find a way out. Paul reassures them that he is not judging or punishing them but rather preparing them (just like God is preparing us) for the kingdom. It reminds me of a song "By and by Lord when the morning comes, all the saints of heaven are gathered home; We will tell the story why we overcome...." Why? Because "we will understand it better by and by." So, when you're in the midst of your trial and tribulation, your particular trial and tribulation, do understand a few things.

Your trial or your tribulation was designed particularly for you by God. Sister Tinelle's tribulation might not be as hard for Sister Christa to handle, and Sister Christa's tribulation might not be as hard for Sister Tinelle to handle. Each trial and tribulation is custom-made for each one of us. And there is another truth that comes with that, and that is that in each tribulation, there is a way out designed for you. There is a reason, and there is a way out. The reason we will know when? By and by. And there is a solution. And the

Each trial and tribulation is **custom-made for each one of us.**

God's Purpose and Plan for your Life

solution is God.

Verse 6 says, "Seeing it is a righteous thing with God to recompense tribulation to them that trouble you." God Himself will repay tribulation such that we do not need to be worrying about that. Rather, God should be glorified in us, and through us is what matters. I remember my lovely wife in the midst of her pain and tribulation; she continued to praise God. You would come over my house and try to comfort her, and before you realized it, she would be asking you how you were doing. She asked you, "how are the kids doing" and "how is your situation improving?" You would be like, "No, no, no. I'm here for you," yet she was always trying to find a way to give God the praise, amen.

We need to use her as an example in our church that we must thank God and praise God in the midst of our trials and tribulations. Now, this is the key, the key to the kingdom, I keep hearing people say. In the midst of your trial, praise Him! When you are going through your trial and tribulation, praise Him. And, when you were laid off at your job, praise Him! People are coming up to you asking how it is going, and you are like, "oh, I'm having a hard time," "I don't know where the Lord is," "the Lord must have left me because my blessings are going downhill," "my unemployment has run out, and

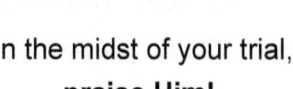

In the midst of your trial, **praise Him!**

I'm about to get kicked out of my town house," and "I've got problems." God may deliver you out of that, but have you truly succeeded at learning and growing in that trial? Have you successfully thanked God and praised God through your trial and tribulation? You have to understand that what is loosed on earth will be loosed in heaven. If sister Tina could, if her body would let her, she would praise God all night long. Her neighbors would be like, "can you please keep it down over there because we are trying to sleep over here." But it's true what is loosed on earth will be loosed in heaven. And the weaknesses that you bind on earth will be bound in heaven, amen?

In verse 7, we read, "and to you who are troubled rest with us, when the Lord Jesus shall be revealed from heaven with his mighty angels, In flaming fire taking vengeance on them that know not God, and that obey not the gospel of our Lord Jesus Christ: Who shall be punished with everlasting destruction from the presence of the Lord, and from the glory of his power." Isn't that, in essence, what the destruction, punishment, and penalty of God are? Its separation from the presence of God.

All our lives, and before we were born, we have always been in God's presence and under God's protection. There has never been a time, sisters and brothers, that you have been without His presence and His protection that comes with His presence. All that He needs to do, like that day on 9/11

God's Purpose and Plan for your Life

when He opened up his hands for a split second, all He needs to do is fall back for a quick second and let you feel what the world is like without Him. That day will come for some but not for us. Thank You, Jesus!

All our lives, and before we were born, we have always been **in God's presence and under God's protection.**

Jesus' Soon and Quick Return

Verse 10 says, "When He shall come to be glorified in his saints and to be admired in all them that believe (because our testimony among you was believed) in that day." Well, Paul is not talking about the rapture, but rather he is talking about Christ's triumphant return in great power and glory at the end of the Tribulation Period that is mentioned in the Book of Revelation. He encourages them and us that we will be a part of that great day, amen? **I'm here to preach to you that Christ's return is soon.**

They have been saying that since forty days after He returned, and ever since then, preachers have been saying to people that same warning that "He is soon to come back." And you say to yourselves, "why do you keep saying that?" There were people that said Jesus was going to come back in 1984.

Sermon 1 – In the Midst

There were people that said He was going to come back in 1999. And, there were some more that said He was coming back in 2000 and 2001. And again, you say, "why, why, why do you say that?" Pastor said, "When God lays a message on your heart, and you don't preach it, then the blood of God's people is on your head, for not preaching God's message to them."

So, I'm telling you that time is winding up, and Christ's return is coming soon. Whenever I tell you Christ is coming soon, it is even more true today than it was when they said those same words over 2,000 years ago! So, when I say to you that our time is winding up and that Christ's return is coming soon, I'm encouraging each one of you to get your own house in order because even next week isn't promised to anyone.

Who's to say that when I was coming up that highway that had I not listened to the Holy Spirit on that road coming back from vacation and I was what caught up in that accident and I was wrapped underneath that metal and burning vehicle, who's to say that was going to be my last day on earth? So, it doesn't matter that Christ didn't technically come back last week, yesterday, or even today. Another interpretation of the word "soon" is "quickly." When the Bible tells us that Christ is coming back soon, it can also be translated that Christ is coming back quickly. So much of the Bible's prophecies have already been fulfilled so that He could return any minute and

God's Purpose and Plan for your Life

be right on time. It is only His grace and His mercy that are allowing us the additional time to get right with Him! If He comes tonight...would you be ready? You might think that you will just pray to God once Jesus cracks the sky, but by then, it will be too late because the Bible clearly tells us that Jesus will come like a thief in the night, and in another scripture, we are warned that He will come in the moment of the twinkling of an eye. No, today is the day of your salvation!

There will come a time when I'm going to be with Him. I will no longer be here to preach anymore, and all of my days and all of my time will be over. So, I have already decided that I'm going to serve the Lord! I'm not trying to scare anybody, but rather I'm just trying to say that whatever God is saying to your heart today, it's for you and for you to act upon. That means if you have an ought with anybody, then forgive them. Remember what we read about today and the church of Thessalonica? They had a love for one another. If you have an ought with anyone in this church, then you need to forgive them because that ought should not be allowed to last. If you have an ought with anyone, it should be an opportunity to either ask for forgiveness or to forgive.

God is telling me tonight to tell His people to drop their rocks. So tonight, we are going to do that. So, I want you to start thinking now about dropping your rocks. Think of those people in this church that you have an ought with; it may be a hidden ought that is buried deep within. If that person is not here when we pray, it's okay; you can still pray for them and keep them in the forefront of your mind.

Although we are going through tough times, hang in there because we have a bright future ahead in God through Christ Jesus. Amen? Glorifying God comes from loving and praising God through our trials and tribulations. How real are our feelings and glorification of God when we haven't gone through anything? I remember that when I really hadn't lost anybody, I didn't know how to write a good sympathy card. If you haven't been through any tough times in your life, then you really might not know how to relate with others who are going through their tough times. Now, since God has taken me through a deep, deep valley experience in my own life, He has taught me how best to relate to those who have lost a loved one; now, I can write with sincerity, touching sympathy cards, and speak honest words of consolation because I've been there, and I've felt those depths.

God's Rewards After Tribulations

Verse 11 says, "Wherefore also we pray always for you, that our God would count you worthy of this calling, and fulfil all the good pleasures of his goodness, and the work of faith with power." Now, remember when we are sitting here and getting

God's Purpose and Plan for your Life

all this good Word, that it's not that the message is for somebody else. God hand-selected exactly who He wanted to be in this service. So, when we are listening, we have to be listening as what thus saith the Lord for us. His word says, "We pray always for you that our God will count you worthy of His calling and fulfill all the good pleasures of his goodness." Can we comprehend all the goodness that God has for us? Can our minds think of all He has in store for us? In 1 Corinthians 2:9, it reads, "But as it is written, Eye hath not seen, nor ear heard, neither have entered into the heart of man, the things which God hath prepared for them that love Him."

Our minds can't comprehend all that God has in store for us. But a lot of the time, those blessings don't get released until we have gone through something. So, if you haven't gone through anything or you haven't gone through it well, you are going to go right back through it again. Keep in mind

God can only do for us all that we **allow Him to do.**

not to try and box God in. God can only do for us all that we allow Him to do. But if we don't give it over to Him and we hold on to it, then it will be like getting back your dirty laundry from the cleaners. So, we have to give it over to the Lord and then find that one way out that He has for us. There is always a ram in the bush, amen? When God closes a door, He always opens a window. Amen?

I'm going to end with 1 Peter 5:10. It reads, "But the God of all grace, who hath called us unto his eternal glory by Christ Jesus, after that ye have suffered a while, make you perfect, establish, strengthen, settle you." May God richly bless each one of you and your families as you find and live out God's Purpose and Plan for your lives!

Sermon 2 – Rock of My Salvation

Verses: 2 Genesis 4:1-7
(Originally preached on March 23, 2003)

"And the Lord said unto Cain, Why art thou wroth? and why is thy countenance fallen? If thou doest well, shalt thou not be accepted? and if thou doest not well, sin lieth at the door. And unto thee shall be his desire, and thou shalt rule over him."

Genesis 4:6-7, KJV

Are we ready for some Holy Ghost good time this morning? It's funny how when you first get saved, you can tap into that power, but very shortly after the realities of life kick in, things change. Somebody said something to you, and it didn't come across right; they raise up their fingers at you, but not all of them go up! Or, they cut you off when you're driving, or somebody gives you trouble on your job about something. You suddenly realize early on that God has given you a situation that has to be managed in your human body, and that's hard. It starts with an indifference where you can kind of take somebody or leave them.

Sermon 2 – Rock of My Salvation

The Bible talks about people being stiff-necked. They don't have a desire to change for the better or to listen to the leading of the Holy Spirit in their lives. Or, maybe they are thinking that they've arrived. Even within the church, there are those who may think that they've arrived, they are saved, and now they feel that they don't need to do anything more. And, then, it mutates into hardness of heart.

The Bible talks about having a hard heart or a stony heart. Jesus must come in and remove that stony heart and replace it with a heart of flesh that He can reach. Left unchecked, their feelings may start to get worse where it creeps into bitterness. How many of us have been bitter towards somebody? Maybe someone in our own family or somebody on our job.

It can end up there because the devil is going to throw things at you because he doesn't know that one thing that's going to affect you. He doesn't know your buttons unless you open your mouth and tell him where your buttons (or pain points) are; other than that, the devil will never know. The devil is just going to keep throwing things at you until that one thing sets you off. And then that leads to hatred.

How deeply can your hatred run for this individual? You get up thinking about him. You say things like, "Grrr, I can't wait 'til I see him again. What am I going to do to him? Before you know it, you start plotting and planning things on what you're going to say. You think to yourself, if he says this to me, then I'm going to say that. And if she says that, then I'm going to come back with this. Today, we are going to talk about a story like this that ends up in bloodshed! If murder goes even further, it can lead to wars because wars have been started over things like this. History shows us that World War I started after the death of one man.

Sin has a process to it, and we are on that track unless we get off through the power of the Holy Ghost. We know that all of God's children have power through the Holy Ghost. God has given us this power, and we must tap into it.

Two Brothers

So, here is the story about two brothers. You would figure two brothers, like two sisters, or a mom and a child, husband and wife are the closest relationships. But how many have you heard this weekend in the news of a man that drowned his four kids? Or, how many of you heard in the news a couple of years back that there was a woman who killed her two boys in a car and drowned them in the lake. So, these are family relationships that should be close, but not all of them are close.

Today's message is about two brothers and begins in Genesis 4, which reads, "And Adam knew Eve, his wife; and she conceived, and bare Cain, and said, I have gotten a man from the LORD. And she again bares his brother Abel. And Abel was a keeper of sheep, but Cain was a tiller of the ground." I looked up these names, and it turns out that Cain means "here

Sermon 2 – Rock of My Salvation

he is" and Abel means "frail." Think about that; how would you feel if your parents named you "here he is" and "frail."

Of course, as we know, there shouldn't be favoritism by the parents between two children, but how many of us know that does happen? Some of us are parents, and we know it's not right, is it? It's not right because it causes jealousy between the children, unnatural jealousy.

To reflect the lack of brotherly love between the two brothers, as an example, let me tell you a quick story about two other brothers that went walking in the woods. As they were walking, a big bear comes out of the forest; this bear was huge! So, they decided let's get running out of here, but immediately the first brother sat down on a stump and started to change into some tennis shoes. He puts his first tennis shoe on, and the other brother is screaming, "What are you doing, man!" At this time, the bear is doing what bears do roaring. And the other brother is saying, "Let's go." Still, the brother is taking his time and putting the other tennis shoe on, tying it real tight." At this point, he hops up and then starts running. As they begin running, the bear begins chasing them. The man asks his brother, why would you take all that time to put on some tennis shoes while this bear is chasing us? Don't you realize that we could have been a little further up the road since you know no one can outrun a bear? The other brother

God's Purpose and Plan for your Life

responds, "I don't have to outrun the bear. I just have to outrun you!" You can have two brothers that don't necessarily have each other's back. That's the way it was with "here he is" and "frail."

Very early on, as parents, we have to learn to be careful and not to favor one child over the other because every child is different. Just because one child has a strength that the other child doesn't have doesn't mean the other child is any less. It just means that they have different strengths and that there is diversity. So, we have to make sure that we encourage our children and our children hear that we love them. A lot of times, we as parents say, "They know I love them." But how many times do we actually verbally say to them, "I love you?" How often do we verbally confirm to our kids that, hey, dad loves you and mom loves you? That is something that we need to remember.

You can have two brothers that don't **necessarily** have each other's back.

We need to love our kids especially during those teen years when their affection level drops and they don't want to be touched, and they don't want to be too close up. It doesn't mean that they don't love us; instead, it just means that they are growing up. We, as parents, have to realize that they are going through different phases, and this is all normal. But it's hard for us parents. We are used to our kids telling us that

Sermon 2 – Rock of My Salvation

they love us.

Kids, you don't realize the connection you have to your parents, but we parents understand. Amen? It's all a part of growing up. Often teens can be less expressive. Prior to their teen years, they would come home and tell us how their day was at school. Now, as teens, they don't want to tell us very much at all. Again, it's not that they don't love us, but rather it's that they're going through a new phase. They may even get upset at us if we try to pry too much into their lives. Still, kids need to remember that it's the job of parents to remain connected in their lives.

Verse 3 says, "And in process of time it came to pass, that Cain brought of the fruit of the ground an offering unto the LORD. And Abel, he also brought of the firstlings of his flock and of the fat thereof. And the LORD had respect unto Abel and to his offering: But unto Cain and to his offering he had not respect."

The difference in the offerings was reflective of the difference in the respect and love for God each of the two men showed that day because God respected Abel and Abel's offering because his offering involved blood and the life of the sacrificial animal. In God's Word, it tells us that without the shedding of blood, there can be no remission for sin.

Trying to Serve God in Distraction

The offering was what each of them gave, the first of their fruit. But let's read this a little closer. It was not only that Cain's offering had no shedding of blood, but also it was how it was brought to God. How many times have you been in church, and you just came out of praise and worship service, yet your mind wasn't on it? Instead, you were thinking about all of the things you have to do after church. When your mind should have been on the Lord, you were thinking, "I have to do this," "I have to pick up that," "I have to get home," and "I got these other things to do."

How many times have you been in praise and worship and thinking about something other than praise and worship? How many times have you been praying, and your mind is thinking about something else? How many times have you been at dinner, and food is smelling wonderful, and you're so hungry, but you know you need to say grace first, and so you say your prayers, but you speed through it? You prayed so fast that halfway through the meal, you're asking yourself, "Did I even pray? Did I say grace?"

How about when you go to bed at night. Ever since you were a child, you were taught to say your prayers before you go to bed. But, how many times have you gotten in bed and you are so tired that saying your prayers is the last thing you're going to do before you go to sleep. Or, sometimes, even if

Sermon 2 – Rock of My Salvation

you're not really tired, and when you start to pray, your sleepiness starts to come on you. You start to pray, and you are like, "Man, I'm getting sleepy," and you can't make it through your prayer.

That might come as a surprise to some. Again, God doesn't always accept our worship. Now that may be a little scary to some of us because we're down here on earth, doing all of the things that we feel a Christian ought to be doing. Then, what happens when we get to heaven only to find out that all of the good things that we thought we had done for the Lord had been done wrong and end up getting burned up. How shocked would we be if none of our good was counted towards us because it was done with the wrong reason or purpose. So, God doesn't always accept our worship and all of our offerings.

> God doesn't always accept our worship. **That might come as a surprise to some.**

Keep in mind; this is the same for the good things which we are doing in the church. I don't know about you, but I work hard for what I do for the Lord, and I want it all to count. I know that I am not the only one; I work hard, and you work hard too. And you don't want to be bringing what you give to God and not getting credit for it.

Doing Things God's Way

Remember when it says, "God loves a cheerful giver." What if you get to heaven and find out every time you gave your tithes and offerings that you didn't give cheerfully? What if you find out every time you gave anything to the church that you didn't do it cheerfully? What if God looks down His Holy ledger and finds out that in your whole life going all the way back from when you first got saved that you had only cheerfully given $1.50! You might think, "But what about all the times I worked overtime to give more money to the Lord, and what about all of the extras that I did for the church?" But God says, "Nope, it didn't count." So, we want to do things, but we want to do it God's way, amen?

In 2 Chronicles 25, there is a story of a king named Amaziah. It states that "he did what was right unto the Lord." Back in those days, Israel was led by various kings in both the northern and southern tribes of Israel. This king was the great-great-great-great-grandson of David. While most of these kings of Israel did not do what was right in the sight of the Lord, king Amaziah was one of only a few exceptions. And God documents all of the kings of Israel in the Bible.

Here is one king of Israel that did things right. However, if you read the story of King Amaziah, you will find that although he did that which was right in the sight of the Lord, unfortunately, he didn't do it with a perfect heart. This illustrates that you can be doing right, but not for the right reasons or not in the right way, and as a result, not getting credit for it. King Amaziah did not get credit because he was not doing it with a perfect heart. We need to come to the Lord with a perfect heart this morning.

> We need to come to the Lord with a **perfect heart** this morning.

Lord, Give Me a Pure Heart

That's why I had you move around and sit in different chairs this morning because I want you to get a different perspective, and I want you to see the church differently. If you're sitting in the same seat, you are probably like, "this is the same old, same old," but I want things to be a little bit different, amen? It's time for us to change our hearts and our minds.

In the Bible, it says that we should have the mind of Christ. "Let this mind be in you that was also in Christ Jesus" (Philippians 2:5, KJV). If you are still going around with your same old mind, still thinking thoughts that you should not, still not caring for the things of God, and so forth, then that change hasn't happened. The question you have to ask yourself is, if there has been no real change in you, then are you really saved? If you still think the same bad thoughts and you still live the same type of life, it makes you wonder.

> The question you have to ask yourself is, if there has been no real change in you, then are you really saved?

That's something that each one of us has to ask ourselves. Repeat after me, "Lord, have I really changed, or do I need to rededicate my life back to you?" Sometimes we may think that we have made a change while we still have one foot in the world and one foot in church. Soon, the one foot in the world starts enticing you to put more than one foot in the world. Before you realize it, you end up having both feet back in the world again, and you know that you need to be cleaned up. You need to be brought back to Jesus' side.

Isaiah 29:13 tells us, "Wherefore the Lord said, forasmuch as this people draw near me with their mouth, and with their lips do honor me but have removed their heart far from me, and their fear toward me is taught by the precept of men." That's the Old Testament. And, in the New Testament, in Matthew 15:8, it says it again, "This people draweth nigh unto me with their mouth, and honoureth me with their lips; but their heart is far from me." And for further confirmation it says it in Mark 7:6, "As it is written, this people honoureth me with their

Sermon 2 – Rock of My Salvation

lips, but their heart is far from me."

What you say and how you live out your life here may not matter because you can tell me anything. You can tell me that you did this, and you did that when only God knows what you do behind closed doors. He knows what you're thinking, and He knows how you act with your husband, your wife, your children, and those closest to you. What if we were to pull up on this screen behind us a video of everything that you're thinking? Just for one day, every thought and every temptation that comes into your mind would be broadcasted for all of us to see. We would see every sin that you think about, all of the faults that you meditate on, and even every temptation that you ponder. Even if you didn't actually go out and do them, just the thoughts that were entertained in your mind may be sin!

Do you think you would want people in this church to see what's really going on inside of you? If you don't want that, don't you realize that God sees it all. God sees every thought and deed. So, it's kind of hypercritical to God and harmful to your own heart to sit up here and smile at me while you know that in a few minutes, you're going to act any kind of way as soon as you walk out of the church. Some may not even plan on waiting until Monday but already have made plans in their minds to commit sins right after church. As soon as you walk out of here, your mind rolls back to the old you. You may think, "I've paid my dues for God, so now I'm going to go out here and do for me." We can't live that way.

Why can't we live that way? Because we were bought with a price. Time is winding up, and if we keep thinking that we have plenty of time, we've rolled back to our old way of thinking. We are not going to do that, are we? That's the lifestyle that we came out from. We must seek to think with the mind of Christ. It's not what our lips are saying; instead, it's the closeness of our heart to God. How many of us truly want to be close to God? How many of us want pure hearts?

> **Why can't we live that way?** Because we were bought with a price.

Verse 6 says, "And the LORD said unto Cain, why art thou wroth? And why is thy countenance fallen? If thou do well, shalt thou not be accepted? and if thou doeth not well, sin lieth at the door." Sin lay at the door like a crouching lion, ready to pounce. How many of you have seen in nature shows how lions crouch really low and become completely silent, quietly walking up within about fifteen feet of their prey right before they take off, running after them and pouncing on them. That's how sin comes at us. Sin doesn't come in, kicking down the door, saying, "Hey, here I come." Instead, it sneaks up and creeps up on you when you least expect it.

Sometimes sin can creep up on you when you're asleep.

Sermon 2 – Rock of My Salvation

You're lying there, and your mind is kind of empty and without thoughts, and the next thing you know, "boop," something sinful pops in your mind. You think to yourself, "Where did that come from? I wasn't even thinking about this person or this situation? I wasn't thinking about it, so where did that thought come from?" The source may be the world, the flesh, or the devil just slipping little, vain, and unwanted thoughts into your mind. It could be something you saw on TV right before you went to sleep. But whatever it is, that negative thought gets in there. What do you do?

Do you entertain it, do you give it a place in your mind, or do you dismiss it and say, "Devil get behind me, in Jesus' name?" We have to realize that we are on the defensive, and we are in a battle that we have to win. The good news is that we are already victorious! We just have to claim what is ours to claim. Our biggest defense is Jesus. Remember, the lion is at the door, ready to pounce on us, right? That's what God told Cain. And keep in mind the timing of this. He told Cain this before Cain had done anything. What He has basically done is shown Cain the two choices that all of us face. "If you do well, won't good things come your way? And if you do bad, isn't sin crouching

> We are in a battle that we have to win. The good news is that we are **already victorious!**

at the door waiting for you?" That's the same choices that we have. We have to make a decision as to which of the two we are going to be, a sinner who does not choose God or a sinner saved by God's grace. We have to come to God with right mind.

Luke 18:9-14 recounts a story of Jesus, and I know you know this story, but let's read it slowly and see what we can pull out of it. It reads, "Also, He spoke this parable to some who trusted in themselves that they were righteous, and despised others." Let's slow that down. He is telling a story to some people that think they're righteous, church folk. He's talking to church folk, but those church folks who despise other people. Didn't we start off talking about how sin creeps in? It starts out with indifference, and then it goes to stiff neckedness. And it goes on and on until, finally its leads to bloodshed, murder, and war. That's what happens to church folk that despise people! Doesn't that seem strange to you that church folk is despising other people? And Jesus takes the time to get them right. So, if you despise someone, you're in the right place.

A Pharisaical Spirit

Let Jesus talk to you this morning. It says, "Two men went up to the temple to pray, one a Pharisee." Now, let's bring this up to date because we don't have modern-day Pharisees, but today we have some church folk with pharisaical spirits.

It continues, "and the other a tax collector." In place of a tax collector, let's say a used car salesman or think of some other person that most people don't think too highly of. The Pharisee stood and prayed thus with himself, "God, I thank You that I am not like other men—extortioners, unjust, adulterers, or even as this tax collector." Okay, so what has he done? He has lifted himself up above somebody else. And he doesn't even know this man or how close this man's heart is with God. So, he has already judged this man probably based on what the man was wearing, or maybe he knows where he works. The Pharisee continues saying, "I fast twice a week; I give tithes of all that I possess." This sounds like a man who thinks he can earn his way into heaven. Basically thinking, "I've done these things for you, so bless me now, because you owe me."

Now let's look at this other man, the tax collector, who is standing afar off. He doesn't even know that he has a right to be in church. He is standing at the back door. "And the tax collector, standing afar off, would not so much as raise his eyes to heaven, but beat his breast, saying, 'God, be merciful to me a sinner!'" How many of us feel like that, calling upon God's mercy and grace every day? That's what keeps us humble, and that's what keeps our minds stayed on God. That's what draws our hearts closer to Him and makes us value God. Remember the story of the ten lepers that Jesus had just healed that walked away. Only one of the lepers came back after Jesus had healed him, and the leper thanked Him.

God's Purpose and Plan for your Life

Only one came back. And Jesus said the one that was forgiven the most loved the most!

When we realize all that we have been forgiven, that's when we truly love the Lord. We are coming out of the Easter season realizing all that Jesus had to endure for us, including the beatings, cursing, spitting, floggings, and then finally the crucifixion, all for our sin; that was a price that we should've had to bear. Then, you realize you have been forgiven of it all, and you love Jesus all the more. And you don't want there to be any distance from you to Him.

> Then, you realize you have been forgiven of it all, and you love **Jesus all the more.**

I remember the song Grace and Mercy, whose lyrics go, "Your grace and mercy, has brought us through; I'm living this moment, because of You. I want to thank You and praise You too; Your grace and mercy brought me through!" Hallelujah!

When we stop what we are doing and meditate on all that Jesus is doing for us and all that God is blessing us with moment by moment, that's when we start to realize that we have to get right with the Lord…and stay right with Him! When sin comes at our door because the devil has crept in unaware, it's our job to resist sin, realizing the devil's tricks. It's not for you to fight devil. Your job is to realize that the devil is bigger than you, and he knows things that you don't know. But, even more

Sermon 2 – *Rock of My Salvation*

importantly, you have to realize that you have a Savior in front of you. I'm talking about backup! If someone comes to your door to cause you trouble, you have someone bigger who has your back! How many of us have had that type of situation? Someone who had your back when you were outnumbered. That's what you have here. Jesus is your Savior that's bigger than any enemy that can come knocking at your door. If anything comes to your door that is too big for you to handle, don't worry about, because Jesus will answer that door for you, amen?

"What a friend we have in Jesus. All our sins and griefs we bear. All because we do not carry everything to God in prayer." That's a simple song, and we all know it. But how many times are we singing a song and thinking about when the football game is going to start? We don't really get it into our spirit. Think about the words of the song now. "All our sins and griefs WE bare," because we don't have enough common sense to take it to Jesus and to let Him handle it. Whenever you have problems, put them in His inbox, let go of them entirely, and then let Him handle it because that's His job and not ours. Let's not try to do His job, but instead, let Him do His job.

When problems come along, so what is our part? James 4:7-8 encourages us, "submit yourselves therefore to God. Resist the devil, and he will flee from you." So, there is a part that we can do. We can "resist" the devil. We don't have to go into sin with arms wide open, and we don't have to automati-

God's Purpose and Plan for your Life

cally accept every temptation that comes down the line. We've been living long enough to know our own areas of weakness, and we know how the devil generally tends to come at us. For someone, it could be lying, while for someone else, it could be a problem with inordinate affection, that is, liking another much more than you should. You notice what the devil does. It's our job to keep the devil far from us and to keep our minds focused on Christ. We are in this battle to resist the devil, and not to entertain evil thoughts, and not to just allow the devil to inundate us.

Verse 8 says, "Cain talked with Abel, his brother: and it came to pass, when they were in the field, that Cain rose up against Abel his brother and slew him." He killed him. "And the Lord said to Cain, where is Abel thy brother? And he said I know not: Am I my brothers' keeper?" The wording is a little strange, so you have to put it in the modern-day way of talking. It's like Cain was saying to God, "It's not my job, Lord, to watch out for my brother…that's Your job. Since it's Your job to keep Abel, why are You asking me where my brother is?" Not only was Cain a murder, but now he is trying to hide the murder by being smart with God.

There wasn't anybody else to blame it on. On the entire earth, there was only Cain and Abel out in that field that day, all by themselves. Why would God ask Cain that question? It's the same phraseology where God came to Adam and Eve and asked, "who told you that you were naked?" Of course,

Sermon 2 – Rock of My Salvation

Almighty God already knows the answer before He asks the question, but what God is doing by asking the question is giving Cain the opportunity to get himself right. It's as if God is saying to Cain, "You messed up, but I want to get our relationship back, so, I'm giving you the opportunity to tell the truth." Cain might have responded, "Yea, I did it! I was upset that my parents were treating me different than my brother and then You come along saying the same thing by saying that my offering was not accepted. I got upset, and then I killed him. I'm sorry, and I shouldn't have done it, but I did it." That's what God was looking for.

Remorse or Repentance

God can work with a heart like that, but as long as you sit there telling a lie upon a lie, blaming others, like Cain did by saying, "It wasn't my fault, God, it was Your fault. It was my parents' fault," then God can't deal with that because these are lies. So, God has to judge the lie without there be any rejoining or re-relating. Cain may have been remorseful for what he did, but there is a difference between remorse and true repentance. You can be driving down the road and get pulled over by the police because you were speeding, justifying it by saying, "I'm late." You were breaking the law. If you are remorseful, you are remorseful that you got caught or that you will have to pay a steep fine or that they are going to take points off your license.

You might be remorseful that because they took the points off your license, your insurance might go up, or probably most of all. You're remorseful because you didn't see the police in time to slow down and were caught speeding. Is that really a repentance? No, that is remorse; that's saying to yourself, "sorry I got caught, sorry that I'll have to pay for the repercussions of being caught." But, all of this does not necessarily mean that there is going to be any real change. You may go away from the experience of learning nothing and thinking to yourself all the while, "You got me this time, but you're not going to catch me next time. I'll have both of my eyes wide open next time."

That's not really repentance. Repentance is acknowledging what you did and then owning up to it by making a U-turn in your thinking and behavior. When our children do wrong, we want them to repent, but remember that our children watch us. And, when our children get to be teenagers, they are actually watching more of what we do than what we say. For example, recently, I actually had to repent myself and come clean with my daughters because I don't regularly gamble in the sense that I would go to Las Vegas and Atlantic City, but whenever the

> Repentance is acknowledging what you did and then owning up to it by making a U-turn in your thinking and behavior.

Sermon 2 – Rock of My Salvation

Mega Millions or Powerball Lotteries would get over 100 million, I'd put a dollar in. It's just a one and a "bazillion" chance, but I thought you never know. Now, what message am I sending my two daughters about gambling? I didn't realize it, but my actions were saying one thing to my daughters while my mouth was saying another. Christa (my oldest daughter) has her permit and can't wait to drive. How am I going to look her in the eyes and say, "Stay below the speed limit" if I am routinely speeding?

What we need is to be repentant. We are going to start living with the mindset that what we do has repercussions because we want that closeness with God. Now, I realize that we are talking about sin. I know that you may say to yourself, "Sometimes the sin is so big, and it has a stronghold on me. It's bigger than me." I remember when I used to smoke cigarettes, and I had tried desperately to stop smoking, but I couldn't. One night I finally prayed and cried out to God to take control over this habit and this addiction, and the next day the habit was broken, hallelujah!

Someone may be addicted to drinking or to a drug or to lying. And you prepare your heart by saying, "this week, I'm not going to lie," but low and behold, an hour or two later, you tell a lie. Or your addiction may be gossiping. You might be on the phone, and you passed on someone else's business. Test yourself by asking, does gossiping give God glory? Is it a sin to smoke cigarettes? Test yourself by asking does smoking cigarettes give God glory? If you can answer that question (smoking, drinking, drugs, lying, gossiping, etc.) with a pure heart, then you're doing fine, but if not, then there is an area for repentance.

In Jude 1:11, it reads, "Woe unto them! for they have gone in the way of Cain." This is at the entire end of the Bible, so why would God remember something from the first few chapters of the Bible and then mention it again towards the end of the Bible? What was the way of Cain? The way of Cain involves not acknowledging the wrong that he did, lying to God about what he had done, and then excusing his own actions.

Cain had a heart full of hatred, jealousy, envy, and anger. You may think you are pretty, but there is always going to be someone prettier. You may think you are strong, but there is always going to be someone stronger. Some may get jealous of someone being more successful. Even in the church, you can be jealous of someone who is more successful in the ministry. Hatred, jealousy, envy, and anger are all the ways of Cain. When you worship God, you have to come to God humble. When you humble yourself before God, you will start to realize what you've been forgiven for and just how thankful you truly are. The one that has been forgiven the most by Jesus and came back is the one that loved Jesus the most.

Now, let's all close our eyes and bow our heads as we come before the Lord one more time. With our eyes closed and our heads bowed, think about our walk with the Lord and the closeness of our heart with the Lord. For those who have drifted a little yet know you are saved, but you just don't feel that closeness with God anymore that you once had, I want you to come to the altar, and I'm going to pray for you. I want you to look inward to yourself and not look at anyone else. I want you to think about all that Jesus has done for you throughout your life. If you feel like there has been this disconnect lately and you have to have that connection back, come now to the altar, and I'm going to pray for you.

For those of you still sitting in your seats, please pray for those who have been obedient to the leading of the Holy Spirit and have come up here to the altar for prayer.

Sermon 3 – His Path to Our Spiritual Recovery

Verses: Ephesians 3:16-19
(Originally preached on September 28, 2003)

"That He would grant you, according to the riches of His glory, to be strengthened with might by His Spirit in the inner man; That Christ may dwell in your hearts by faith; that ye, being rooted and grounded in love, May be able to comprehend with all saints what is the breadth, and length, and depth, and height; And to know the love of Christ, which passeth knowledge, that ye might be filled with all the fulness of God."

Ephesians 3:16-19, KJV

It's good that we read God's Word together. Last time I came before you, I reminded you that research finds that you only remember 30 percent of what you hear, 60 percent of what you read, yet 90 percent of what you do and speak. What you do, you will remember 90 percent of it. So, we're going to read God's Word together, but remember that it is more importantly to do it!

Sermon 3 – His Path to Our Spiritual Recovery

In Ephesians 3:16-19, it tells us "That He would grant you, according to the riches of his glory, to be strengthened with might by his Spirit in the inner man; that Christ may dwell in your hearts by faith; that ye, being rooted and grounded in love, may be able to comprehend with all saints what is the breadth, and length, and depth, and height; And to know the love of Christ, which passeth knowledge, that ye might be filled with all the fulness of God."

I apologize to the pastor. When I spoke on the phone, I told him that this message was coming out of the book of Romans. But, as it turned out, the Holy Spirit has led me to the book of Ephesians today. To understand today's scripture, we first have to understand that the trials, tests, and tribulations we go through are for the perfecting of our spirit. In this case, perfection means completing. Through this life, God is perfecting or completing our closeness to Him and our walk with the Lord.

Isn't it strange the phrases that sometimes we Christians say out of our own mouths? Do we ever think about how strange we might sound to the world? We might say things like, "oh Lord, perfect me," "Lord, make me mature in you," or "Lord, I want to know You in the fellowship of Your suffering." Do we really know what we are asking for, or, if so, do we really want that? Be careful what you ask for because the Lord just may give it to you.

In the Fellowship of His Suffering

In this Christian life and in this maturing process, we go through stuff. We ministers go through stuff too, and our pastor goes through stuff as well. We all go through stuff. Take, for instance, that there I was preparing for today's message, but guess where all of my sermon notes ended up? They were at home, yet I was two hours away in Breezewood, PA, and I couldn't get back. I could've stressed out or blamed the situation or others. But it was at that very moment that I received reassurance that everything was going to be okay. Why? Because it was then that God reminded me that His revelation and the truths of His Word are revealed to His saints in His time...not ours. I learned that day that it is not in all of my Christian help and resources that I have at home. It's not in how long I study. It's not even in how much effort I put into it. It's all in God's Word and in His revelation.

As I study God's Word and as I live out the many experiences that He blessed me with so far, that's when His revelation comes. That is what tonight's sermon is about. It might sound a little bit different, but that's okay, amen?

First, let's start out by recounting what we talked about two weeks ago. We talked about the importance of our tes-

Sermon 3 – His Path to Our Spiritual Recovery

> It is that testimony that is **our first and most powerful message.**

timony. We talked about how each of us has our own testimony about the day we were saved and born again. And, it is that testimony that is our first and most powerful message of invitation to strangers we encounter along the way, who may be seeking to find Jesus.

Some of us maybe haven't blown the dust off our testimony or even thought about that glorious day in a long time. Still, each of us has a unique testimony of the special day that changed our lives forever.

Testimonies are unique, but there is one thing that is common to them all, and that is that someone else preached or spoke or led us to Christ... no one arrived saved and born again all by themselves. This underscores the necessity for us to evangelize and tell the Good News of the gospel of Jesus Christ...not by quoting scores of Bible scriptures, but instead by telling others how Jesus saved one person...you!

> No one arrived saved and born again all by themselves.

A while back, we actually did an exercise where we went around the room, having everyone paired up and then having each pair give their testimony to their partner. During these testimonies, they went back in their minds and recounted that faithful day when the Lord spoke to their hearts, one on one. The funny thing was that there were some that could remember the actual date of their salvation, while there were others that couldn't remember the date.

There were some that could remember what they were wearing, where they were, or which friends were with them, while some could not. But each and every one of us had some memory of that faithful day. For those of you who missed out, after the testimonies, we talked and shared about the importance of being ministers to others. We emphasized that the word minister simply means servant, and therefore, this important work of ministering or serving others cannot happen without us.

We have to remember that oftentimes we are the only Bible that the world will ever be read, so if we do remember that day and what we felt that day, then we must share it.

So, let's go around the room and let me hear what you felt on the day of your salvation. If you had to encapsulate your testimony, what would be the one emotion that you were feeling that day. Anybody? Speak up because I have a whole bunch of them, and you don't want me to talk the whole time.

Go ahead, Danielle. You say that you were a little scared. Anyone else? Grandma Gay, you say that you were grateful. I like that. Nicole, you say that you were cold. Brother Dallas?

Sermon 3 – His Path to Our Spiritual Recovery

Brother Dallas says that it was raining, but he felt good. Does anyone have any other positive emotions that they remember? Words like "free," "happy," and "excited" quickly come to mind. Now you're talking. I'm liking what you're saying because if it's a real feeling or a real emotion, then it really gets to you...that's it! Then, with some, you don't really have words for it. There is no one answer because just as unique as our testimonies are, so are our reactions and feelings of that special day.

> Just as unique as our testimonies are, so is our reactions and feelings of that special day.

If I had to try and capture what each and everyone was saying in their own way was that **step one** on that day, there was an acknowledgment of our sin and that we began to look at ourselves in an all-new way. **Step two**, we felt free because all of that nastiness was lifted off of us—hallelujah! That result was feeling "overjoyed," "happiness," "zeal," and "love." What happens to us, though? We remember that day, and we remember those emotions, but that day something changes. Afterward, we go back out into the world, but we continue to feel good inside; because we feel empowered, we feel that we are saved. Cici now feels that she has everlasting life—praise God!

There was an email that someone sent me, and I don't remember all the words, but it starts off by saying, "Thank You,

God's Purpose and Plan for your Life

Lord, that I haven't hollered at anyone today. Thank You, Lord, that I haven't cut someone off today." The e-mail message continues through a list of similar thank you's, but then the writer cuts himself off by saying, "Well, I haven't gotten out of bed yet, but be with me throughout the day!" We can be very sanctified in our own bedroom, in our home, and even in our church among our church family, but the challenges aren't in here. They are out there in the world.

There are times in our lives where we don't feel entirely connected with God. We feel like something has changed. But, how many of us know that when it comes to God, change is not part of Him. We serve an unchanging God. In Malachi 3:6, God says, "I am the Lord, I change not." God doesn't change because He doesn't need to…He is always right. So, if we know that God doesn't move away from us and that God doesn't change, then if we feel that we are now feeling more distant from God, then who moved? We did!

It may be a result of something we have done, or it may be that we are not studying our Word like we should, even though we know better. You know that we've been well trained to read our Word at Tree of Life Bible Church. We are Tree of Life Bible Church, with the emphasis

> We know that God doesn't move away from us and that God doesn't change, then if we feel that we are now feeling more distant from God, then who moved? **We did!**

61

Sermon 3 – His Path to Our Spiritual Recovery

on "Bible Church," and it is here that we encourage the saints to study God's Word regularly and to grow in Bible knowledge.

Still, sometimes things happen, life gets busy, and life gets complex. You might have been sent on travel for work, or you may have had an illness in your family, or just something or someone has started taking your focus temporarily off of God, and you feel it. I don't know about you, but I'm going to speak for myself. There were times when I was sent on travel for work for a week at a time. Because I have to leave on a Sunday, literally I missed an entire week's worth of church services, and I could feel it. Whenever I would return back to church, I would feel less connected...I felt like something was just off.

We have all felt like that at one time or another. Amen? Like I mentioned earlier, God hasn't moved, so it's up to us to get back in alignment with Him. Even if the path back to Him is not always easy, we have to find our way back to God.

When we look at verse 16, it says, "That He would grant you, according to the riches of His glory." How much glory does He have? It says, "Riches of His glory." He is saying that there is no limit to God's glory. There is a worldly perspective that the more I give to you, the less I have. That's what the world teaches us...it encourages us to go out, to make money, and then to hold on to our money tightly, but that is not God's way.

The World Through God's Eyes

God's heavenly paradigm is different because heaven has no limitations. God has no limitations to the amount of His glory, His power, His strength, or His might, and there is no limit to how much of it He can give out to each of us. Do you understand what that means to you? I heard some Christians pray saying, "Father, give my blessing to Sister Donna." Is God that limited to where He has only one blessing to give either to me or to you? No! God knows that the more He gives, the more there is. That's the opposite of the world's paradigm. If we see only with the world's eyes, then we can only see that the more we give, the less we have. But, when we start to see this world with God's eyes, then we will realize that the more He gives us, and the more we give to others, then the more we will get.

We start off in this world feeling clean, but then sin comes along and takes our eyes and our focus off of the Lord. We start to feel the burdens of guilt and the yokes of sin. But praise God that He Himself has given us a method for breaking yokes and lifting burdens. We know that God loves us, and He will never let us go. We need to get back on His path of spiritual recovery.

Well, let me start off by asking the question, is everyone saved? I have great news. And it's not that I saved a lot of money getting Geico insurance. It is good news because everyone here tonight has raised their hands that they are saved,

Sermon 3 – His Path to Our Spiritual Recovery

and since you are saved, then you are already on God's path. There should never be a person that says to you, "I've sinned, I've backslidden, I have fallen out of alignment with the Lord, and now there is no hope for me." Everyone that is a child of God is on God's path. Amen. Thank God!

God's own almighty power places us on the path, and no power on earth can remove us from His path. Romans 8:38-39 tells us that nothing can separate us from the love of God. In that same way, no man can remove us from God's path, no boyfriend and no girlfriend, no husband and no wife, no job, and no temptation. I thank God for his power. I used to lead a song in the choir that said, "I'll climb the highest mountain, and I'll cross the deepest sea whatever the cost, whatever the cost, I will find you, Lord." However, we know it is not God who is lost. We don't need to climb the highest mountain or search the deepest sea. He has not moved. He was God in the beginning, He is God right now, and He will be God in the end, amen?

In reality, it is us who have moved, and it is God who finds us. It is He who puts us on His path. It is important to note that whatever state that He finds us in, we are not so low that God can't lift us up. Verse 16 says, "To be strengthened with might by his Spirit in the inner man."

When we are down and disconnected and feeling that we are to be strengthened with God's might, through His Holy Spirit, our inner man, it is our God who steps right in! When we are feeling out of alignment with God, you have to ask yourself, what part of us is out of alignment? What part of us is it that feels that disconnected? It is our spirit...our inner man. It is God who puts our spirit in us and God who will fix it up. It is God who guides our feet and directs our steps all along His path to recovery.

Different Stages On God's Path

We may all be on God's path. We may all be on God's path, however we may all be at different stages in our Christian walk. Some of us may have known the Lord for many years, but we feel less clean. We may have used words we wish we could take back. Or, maybe we've said or done something that we feel is too far back, or maybe it is something that we did today. We may have spoken a lie this evening on our way to church, or maybe we even cursed someone out in the past hour, or maybe we lost our temper within the last five minutes. Because we never know at what stage another Christian brother or sister may be at in their journey with the Lord, this should lead us to have patience with all those in the church because we remember when we

> We may all be on God's path, however we may all be at **different stages in our Christian walk.**

Sermon 3 – His Path to Our Spiritual Recovery

were at our own earlier stages.

Just that quick, we can feel that disconnected. But, thank God that it is He that brings us back. Some of us may feel that we are progressing on His path, while others might not. When you look around the church, you may even feel that some of the saints are growing closer and closer to the Lord while others are being blessed upon blessed. It's at moments like this that you may ask yourself, "why is that not happening to me?" "why is it that my car is always breaking down?" "why am I always the one being held back on a promotion?" "why is it me all the time?" You may even ask yourself, "why am I not happy in the Lord like I used to be?"

In this evening's scripture, it says, "that Christ may dwell in your hearts by faith; that ye, being rooted and grounded in love." Now think about the phrase "rooted and grounded." I didn't have all of my pastoral resources available to me, so I couldn't look up these Greek and Hebrew words for their additional meaning, but I will tell you that grounded is a term that they used back then for building foundations to walls in buildings. It gave the connotation of digging down through the loose soil and sand until you got to some bedrock. They did this because they didn't have cement like we have today, and if they couldn't find bedrock to build on, they were out of luck, and their houses would fall! So, they would just have to keep on digging and digging until they hit bedrock. That's grounded.

Rooted talks about the same concept but from a slightly

different approach. The reference for rooted comes more from agriculture and trees. Roots go way down, so this word gives the connotation of stability and feeding. Trees are fed through the roots, so if someone ever wanted to kill a tree, all they would have to do is to cut off its roots.

Our way to recovery is going to involve getting down deep to our foundation and constantly being fed. What makes me disconnected when I'm away, may be that I am not being fed the Word of God. I can be reading God's Word and still feel like I'm not being fed. How can that happen? Maybe, you are regularly studying your Word, but you are forsaking the assembly of the brethren. Touch your neighbor and tell them, "We need each other!" Sometimes we need each other more than our own words can say. I need to see you, sister, I need to see your smile, I need to hear your testimony, I need to feel that you are approachable, I need to feel free to be able to come up to you and say, "please pray for me," and I need to know that you will actually do it! More importantly, what can I pray about for you? Thank God that God blessed us with Christian friends. There is that heart-to-heart closeness here at this church that is not pretentious or phony. I have a joy when I see you; my whole day cheers up; you're my buddy, and like Brother Rob is fond of saying, "We roll like donuts!"

If it is true that cleanliness is next to godliness, then when we start to feel dirty, full of sin, deprived, and dejected, what can we do? For Martin Luther, when he looked at himself, he

Sermon 3 – His Path to Our Spiritual Recovery

said, "I'm nothing but a worm." When he looked at the depravity of his own heart, he couldn't describe it in a way that would be equal to that of a person. The only thing he could equate it with was a lowly worm...not something you could boast about. Worms are blind and eat dirt. That's what he thought about himself.

In Philippians 3:4-8, we see that the apostle Paul took it a step further when he described himself as an inanimate thing, even lower than a worm. He starts off by saying," If you count all of my benefits," and then he goes down a list of them, including a Hebrew of Hebrews, born of the stock of Israel and circumcised on the eighth day. He's telling you of all of his accolades, yet when he gets down to the bottom, he says," I count it all dung." Many churches were planted during Paul's ministry, and yet, when he looked at himself, all he could describe it as was "dung." I'm not even a worm, but instead, all I am is some poop on the ground.

Remember, cleanliness is next to godliness, right? The good news is we have been strengthened by what? God's own might. It's our belief that God has all might. Through God's strength, Matthew 21:21 and Mark 11:23 remind us that if we say to the mountain to move, then that mountain would jump up and cast itself into the sea, amen? If that's the might that God has, and God is blessing us with strength from His might, then as the prophet Jeremiah says in Jeremiah 32:17, "there is nothing too hard for God," and like Apostle Luke tells

God's Purpose and Plan for your Life

us in Luke 1:37 "there is nothing impossible for Our God to do." Do we really believe that? We say things like "God blessed me with strength this week." Because I'll tell you how we use it in a sentence, and you tell me if I'm right. We would say something like, "Child, that girl rolled her eyes at me, and I was about to get her told. But thank God He gave me strength this week."

In times like that, am I allowing God's strength to replace my weakness? No. What if you are in a situation where you might see someone looking at you cross-eyed. At first, you may play it off thinking, "Okay, whatever. Maybe they're having a bad day." But then you turn back and look again, and they're still looking you up and down. And you might want to go over there and say something to them, but God's might can move mountains, amen? Soon, we may see we are not very clean at all.

Verse 17 says, "That we may be able to comprehend with all saints." What are we comprehending? It's beautifully written. It's very poetic. Sometimes we get lost in the poetry of God's Word just like in the scripture Philippians 4:8 that reads, "Finally, brethren, whatsoever things are true, whatsoever things are honest, whatsoever things are just, whatsoever things are pure, whatsoever things are lovely, whatsoever things are of good report; if there be any virtue, and if there be any praise, think on these things." God wrote that. So, what does this mean here?

Sermon 3 – His Path to Our Spiritual Recovery

What are we talking about here? "The breadth, and length, and depth, and height" that we are talking about is the love of God through Christ Jesus, amen? All throughout the Sunday Morning message, the pastor preached to us about agape. This is agape…it is God's type of love, and it is unconditional! God's spiritual recovery allows us to increase our strength that is given to us through His might. His might prevents us from using our strength wrongly.

God warns us in Ephesians 4:26 to "Be angry, and sin not." The strength of God gives strength to our inner man. When we feel our lowest, that's when we know that it is God's might strengthening us. Now that we know about God's strength let's take a closer look at His love…that agape love. This is the love you get that you don't deserve. That's the love that God gives you. Remember that after we have done wrong, we need to get on His road to recovery, and we need to get back to doing right. We need to get back to being right not because of Him but because of us. We don't want to feel disconnected anymore.

A Personal Testimony

When I was fifteen years old, I got saved and born again on a cool evening in July. I had put it off as long as I could because I knew God's voice was talking to me, even though I was a kid. I fought it, and fought it, and fought it. I remember all of my friends were getting saved, and I saw the positive reaction within each of them. At first, I thought they were faking it, and I'm like, "What's that about?" But it was real, and when it was my turn, I remember standing as far away from the crowded tabernacle as I could...Actually, I was standing outside! Still, I could hear that the preacher kept saying, "There is one more person out there that wants to be saved." We have been in services like this, right, where a pastor says that, and we might be tempted to think to ourselves, "Man, pastor is milking it" or "Doesn't he realize that I've got chicken to get in the stove and I don't have time for this."

It is at these times that God's Holy Spirit is stirring something up in that pastor's spirit. On a spiritual level, the pastor can actually look out into the congregation and tell that there is one more child of God whose spirit is yearning. You may want to come up, but be fearful or have a quenching of the spirit holding you back. I pray that I never rush a sermon so much that I won't wait for that one person that truly wants to be saved because I was that one person. I swear it felt like twenty or twenty-five minutes.

He was a very highly respected preacher, so no one was moving to the altar, perhaps out of fear. So, I turned and went the other way like I was Jonah. This particular church building was a long slender building, and I made my way all the way to the back of the church and then actually outside. But still, I knew it was God's voice talking to me. I was outside the

Sermon 3 – His Path to Our Spiritual Recovery

church chatting it up with my friends, but all the while, this man of God was talking, and all I could clearly hear was God speaking to me...but it wasn't in my ears. Can anyone relate to what I'm talking about? I heard God speak to me personally, and He made Himself quite clear. That was the end of me deciding what I was going to do. I got up there as fast as I could, and I thank God that He accepted me and that I was saved that day.

There is a battle going on, and the battle is in that inward man. We know that we sin, and we know that some may feel like they sin more than others. There may be some that may be doing drugs, or some that may be having sex outside of the union of marriage. God gave me this message to preach, and I'm not going to sugar-coat it. It's not going to be on my head. There may be someone that could be stealing today or someone breaking the law some other way. But sin is sin in God's eyes. Sometimes we think that some sin is worse than others or sometimes we feel that our sins aren't that bad. We might even be tempted to think, "I know what this person is doing, so my sin is not that bad." But God says no. Sin is sin. Sin is defined as separation from God. So, that day when I was fifteen, and He joined Himself to me through Christ, and an eternity relationship was re-established—thank God!

When you sin, sometimes you know it's a sin, and you feel bad about it. You know God is watching you, but still, you go ahead and sin anyway. God loves us with His agape love, and

God's Purpose and Plan for your Life

He loved us before we sinned. He loved us before we were saved. He loved us before we were saved. He loved us before we were born! God sent his only Son to die for you before your grandmother was born! Do you honestly think that something you did today or yesterday separates you from Him? Do you honestly think that God didn't know that you were going to do that today? We know that Christ lives in our hearts through faith.

He loved us before we were saved. **He loved us before we were born!**

Also, we know that in our hearts are other things. Hatred dwells in there. Racism dwells in there. Deceitfulness, jealousy, envy, and scorn can all live in there. And, on top of that, there is the devil that does nothing all day but goes back-and-forth to the Lord, showing Him all of our faults. We have a Christ who has paid the full propitiation or full payment for our sin. We know that the sin that has been forgiven is a sin with a capital "S." What does that mean? That means all sin! The sin you're going to do tomorrow and the bad thoughts you are going to think tonight in bed, He has already forgiven you—hallelujah! Jesus Christ has already died for those sins and more. When you start to think about the height of your sin, the lowness of your depravity, and then think about this, that you "may be able to comprehend with all saints what is the breadth, and length, and depth, and height; And to know the

Sermon 3 – His Path to Our Spiritual Recovery

love of Christ, which passeth knowledge."

We say that we can comprehend because comprehending means knowing, yet this knowing involves two things. First, comprehending involves **learning**. You go to school to learn things. So, if you're ever going to comprehend something tonight, it's because first, you learned it.

My mom is a teacher, and we had some time to talk on this long trip. I was telling her that I thank God for her and the other teachers in my family. When I came out of college, I thought I was going to do this and be that, but I found that through my career, a lot of the stuff that we think is so important later on doesn't mean a thing. A few weeks back. I had to clean out my office because they were putting in new carpet. So, we had to put all of our things in boxes and put them away, and then weeks later, we would take them back out. But when we decided to clean our office, many of my co-workers and I decided that all of the old stuff can go. We threw away all of these old manuals for technologies that we had learned and didn't use anymore.

But when you consider a teacher, they are investing in the mind of a child. When they plant that seed in a child, that young seed begins to grow. It could be a seed for good or a seed for bad, but that seed will grow, and when it grows, they have impacted the path that one child takes. They have also impacted all the people the child grows up with and interacts with.

God's Purpose and Plan for your Life

When I was young, I was taught the saying "early to bed, early to rise, makes a man healthy, wealthy, and wise." And throughout my life, I found it to be true. Early bird does seem to always get the worm. If I instill that in you, and you instill that in the next generation and so forth, you can see how this small seed can grow. There is a learning process. Thank God that there are teachers.

Paul tells us in Acts 2:47 that God "sends to the church such as needed." One of the things He sends to churches are teachers because He knows that we all need to learn, but there is more to comprehending than learning, and that's experiencing. The second part of comprehending is **experiencing**. We must experience what we've learned. How do you experience this agape love and the breadth, and length, and depth, and height of it? It is to know the love of Christ, which passeth all knowledge, that ye might be filled with all the fulness of God.

I say to you there is no way for us to fully comprehend without experiencing it. When we use those phrases such as, "Lord, let me grow closer to you," "I want to walk with you," "I want to be your friend," and "I want to know you in the fellowship of your suffering" be careful what we ask for. I will tell you this. I have suffered over the past two years to the point where I wouldn't wish what has been on me on anybody else. But, in the same breath, I will tell you this, now that I'm on the other side of it and through my valley experience, I thank God for it.

Sermon 3 – His Path to Our Spiritual Recovery

Even though it's a hard thing to say.

I can even remember before this suffering happened to me that I was not one of those ones who would get up in the pulpit and say, "I want to know you in the fellowship of your suffering." But when you get to know Christ, the things that were important to you before are not that important to you anymore.

A 19th century American named Edward Payson referred to the stages of Christian development using an image of Jesus surrounded by four concentric circles. Without going into a lot of detail, he found that the ones that were the closest to Jesus Christ were characteristically humbled, outwardly blessed, and rich in walking with Christ.

However, this message that God gave me tonight is not for that circle. This message is for the remaining three circles. These are the Christians that are characterized as being caught up in the distractions of life that usher in sin. This sin may come in as the littlest of sin, but soon they work in separating us from Christ and taking our focus off Christ, and before we know it, we begin to do something that is devastating to Christians…compromise.

You can be on your job and think, "I can steal this stapler because it's only worth $10" or "it's an old stapler, and the company is probably going to throw it away anyway." You might be further tempted into thinking, "I really do need a stapler, and

I don't have the $10...." That's called compromise! Compromise is trying to live with one foot on the Lord's side and the other foot on the world's side. Earlier I described the difference between heaven's paradigm and the world's paradigm and seeing this world through God's eyes or through the world's eyes. These two paradigms don't work in conjunction with each other.

> **Compromise** is trying to live with one foot on the Lord's side and the other foot on the world's side.

Brothers and sisters, remain grounded and rooted in God's Word. Remain on God's path to recovery with the Lord, knowing that the increase in our strength comes from God's might. Remain grounded in God's agape love to fully comprehend the breadth, length, depth, and height of His love that passes all knowledge. And, then, we may be filled with the fullness of God.

Let's stand for the benediction. "Now unto Him who is able to do exceedingly and abundantly above all that we can ask or think, according to His power which is revealed in Him be glory in the church and in Christ Jesus throughout all generations, forever and ever. Amen!" God bless you!

Sermon 4 – The Holy Spirit in Us

Verses: John 16:7-16
(Originally preached on November 28, 2010)

"Nevertheless, I tell you the truth; It is expedient for you that I go away: for if I go not away, the Comforter will not come unto you; but if I depart, I will send Him unto you."

John 16:7, KJV

Praise the Lord, church. Praise the Lord, church! Today's message will come from John 16:7-16. Let's read today's scripture; it begins, "Nevertheless, I tell you the truth; It is expedient for you that I go away: for if I go not away, the Comforter will not come unto you; but if I depart, I will send Him unto you. And when He is come, He will reprove the world of sin, and of righteousness, and of judgment: Of sin, because they believe not on Me: Of righteousness, because I go to my Father, and ye see Me no more; Of judgment, because the prince of this world is judged. I have yet many things to say unto you, but ye cannot bear them now. Howbeit when He, the Spirit of truth, is come, He will guide you into all truth: for He

Sermon 4 _ The Holy Spirit in Us

shall not speak of Himself; but whatsoever He shall hear, that shall He speak: and He will shew you things to come. He shall glorify Me: for He shall receive of mine and shall shew it unto you. All things that the Father hath are mine: therefore, said I, that he shall take of mine, and shall shew it unto you. A little while, and ye shall not see Me: and again, a little while, and ye shall see Me, because I go to the Father."

Now, let me transition over to John 14:16-18, and it says, "And I will pray the Father, and He shall give you another Comforter, that He may abide with you forever; Even the Spirit of truth; whom the world cannot receive, because it seeth Him not, neither knoweth Him: but ye know Him; for He dwelleth with you, and shall be in you. I will not leave you comfortless: I will come to you." May the Lord add a blessing to His already blessed word.

God Living Within You

This morning the message is "The Holy Spirit in you!" A lot of times, when you think about the Holy Spirit, you don't think of it as being in you, and maybe you don't put two and two together and realize that Jesus lives in each of us. We all believe that Jesus came into our hearts, but how many of us know that the Holy Spirit lives in our heart, too? Jesus tells us that He "will dwell with you And I shall be in you." So, you have the Son and the Holy Spirit in you! And, guess what? The father lives within you too, so wherever you go, you have the triune power of God inside of you! wherever you go, you have the triune power of God **inside of you!**

What is the important role of the Holy Spirit in our lives? We talk around the Holy Spirit, but do we know that much about the Holy Spirit? Jesus wants us to know about Him, and He wants us to know all aspects of His father and all aspects of His Holy Spirit. Unfortunately, the Person of the Holy Trinity seems to always drop off the edge. Some people don't really know too much about the Holy Spirit, like who the Holy Spirit is. What we want to do today is take a look at who the Holy Spirit is and is not and what He came to do and not do.

We start off by thinking about who we are…we are sinners saved by grace…we are depraved, and without Jesus Christ living down deep on the inside of us, there is no good thing in us. Sometimes we don't want to look at who we are, but instead, we look at others and say, you're wrong, he's wrong, and she's wrong. But when we actually take a look at ourselves, we realize there is no good thing in us. We think we are all that, and we're not. That's the truth about it.

When we start to see ourselves as God sees us, we start feeling convicted. Now that's one of the jobs of the Holy Spirit…to convict the sin in our lives. Now is it to put us in despair,

Sermon 4 _ *The Holy Spirit in Us*

or is it to drive us into the open arms of Christ? When you were unsaved or when you have backslidden, you wonder why we sit in our seats when altar call comes even though we can hear this voice in our ear, saying go up, go up. The unction of the Holy Spirit is pulling you, and it is encouraging you to repent. And you say what is that?

That's the Holy Spirit speaking to you and driving you into the open arms of Christ Jesus. Thank God once we finally realize that Jesus paid it all. Jesus paid it all! Can I get an Amen? Jesus paid it all. He paid for all of our sins. All of our debts that we couldn't pay, He paid them all off! That's when that relief washes over us, realizing what the Holy Spirit is driving us to do is for our own good.

God's Love Changes Us For the Better

Sometimes people ask me why I do what I do. Why am I always in church on Sunday mornings listening to the preacher preach? Why am I always in church on Wednesday for the mid-week prayer service and Bible study? And for some, why am I always in church on Thursday for choir rehearsal? I know your unchurched family members, neighbors, and friends see you going to church all the time and thinking, "What is up with that?" You say to yourself, "How do I answer that?"

How do I answer why am I always in church? My answer is I believe every word of God is true. What do you believe? Why

God's Purpose and Plan for your Life

are you always here? Is it just for show? No! Is it just because you want to see who else is going to be there? No! We are drawn here to church because the Word of God is true. We believe in every word of prophecy that we can understand. We believe in every miracle that is written in the pages of scripture. Amen?

We believe it. Every word of God is true. If we believe that every word of God is true, we believe that life is but a vapor. We are here today and gone tomorrow. The Bible says we are like grass that is cut down, dried up, and blown away. I also believe that there is an eternity. Our souls were built to live forever, so what do you believe? Now, in our bylaws, there is a list entitled "What We Believe." I believe there is a heaven, I believe there is a hell, and I believe that if we live right and accept Christ on this side of life, then we are going to heaven. We get to live with Him for eternity.

> We are drawn here to church because the **Word of God is true.**

Now, this isn't all that we believe. But this is the beginning of what we believe. What we believe drives what it is we do. When you start to see things the way God sees things, then you don't mind being in church a lot because you start to realize that's where your strength comes from. Why wouldn't I want to learn more about where my strength comes from?

Sermon 4 _ The Holy Spirit in Us

There's a song that Whitney Houston used to sing that says, "where do broken hearts go? Can they find their way home?" The answer is yes. They can find their way home, but they have to find their way home to Jesus. A lot of us lost loved ones in 2010. At this church, we dealt with the passing of one of our own deacons here. In addition, recently, deacon Collins lost his brother.

Each of us has lost someone that really mattered to us in 2010. I looked it up and found how many famous people died in 2010, and they include some singers like Teddy Pendergrass, Marvin Isley of the Isley Brothers, and Teena Marie. Likewise, actors Gary Coleman, Tony Curtis, and Patricia Neal. Also, sausage King Jimmy Dean also died. Even the rich and the famous cannot buy their way out of death. It is an amazing fact that 1 out of every one person dies!

It is an amazing fact that **1 out of every 1 person dies!**

The important thing is that when people die, if that someone that you know is saved, then you know that they are on their way to heaven. They are not lost, they are with Jesus, and so we feel less sad after their passing. We still mourn when they die, but we know their final destination. Similarly, we know that eventually, if we live our lives right and stay saved, then we too will know our destination.

We will see that loved one again. This is a person that,

God's Purpose and Plan for your Life

although they passed on, they believed in that good gospel message, and we will see them again, amen? What is it that we wanted to do in 2011? In 2011, we wanted to get that gospel message out. Because the more people that hear that good gospel message, then hopefully the more people that will believe it. And, the more people that believe it, then the more people that will get saved and born again in Christ!

What You Believe and What You Do

You see how it's important what we believe because it drives what we do and what we have faith in. Before we get to know about the Holy Spirit, we need to know about God. That's why we were placed here on earth. We were placed here on earth to have a relationship with God, but you need to know Him to relate with Him. Does that make sense? Before I can relate to Him, I need to know Him. I need to be able to recognize Him out of any crowd. How would I know which man in a crowd is my dad if I've never seen my dad, don't know what he sounds like, and don't even know what he looks like? I need to be able to know God.

> We were placed here on earth to have **a relationship with God.**

You don't want to get to heaven and not know Jesus because you have never spoken to Him. You don't want to get to heaven and not know God because you haven't prayed. And worst yet, He doesn't know you, and then God turns to you and says, "I never knew you!" No one wants that!

Knowing Who God Is

So, you want to know about God. Once you seek God, then you will find God. In the first place, we know that God is **omniscient**. Have you heard that word before? In fact, when you heard that word, there were two other words with it…omnipotent and omnipresent. They were always said in threes. Like, when they talk about the word love. It's defined in three different words: agape love, eros love, and phileo love.

God is omniscient; that is to say, He knows everything. There is nothing that He knows tomorrow that He didn't know yesterday. He always knows everything. Now that will confuse some people. They may ask themselves, "well, does He know if I'm going to sin tomorrow?" Yes, He knows. God knew it before you were born and before your grandfather was born because when God looks at you, He sees your whole life rolled out like a scroll! When I see you, I see you today? I met you today, I got to know your name, and

> When God looks at you, He sees your whole life **rolled out like a scroll!**

God's Purpose and Plan for your Life

I'm learning a little bit about you because I don't know everything about you. But, when God looks at you, He sees you as a baby, as a young adult, and as an old person all at the same time. He sees your grandbabies and your grandparents all in an instant.

God is also **omnipotent**; that is to say, He is all-powerful. That means there is nothing He cannot do. There is nothing bigger than Him. There is no trial that He can't master because God made it all. Now you say that's good for Him, but how does that help me? It means that there is nothing bigger in your life than God, and you cannot come to Him with a problem that is so big that He can't handle it!

Sometimes you may have a habit...a bad habit. For example, you may be smoking, and you say to yourself, "well, my church brothers and sisters don't know about it." But we don't need to know about it, because more importantly remember that God knows.... God knows everything. So, it doesn't matter what I see and what I know. Whatever you're doing behind closed doors, and whatever you do on Friday and Saturday nights, God knows.

The reality is that God knows our faults, our weaknesses, our bad habits, and our sins, and He is the one who we need to be more concerned about knowing. So, He knows it, and He has the power to remove it if you let Him. We are not robots; we need to ask Him, "Lord, come into my life," "Lord come and handle this situation...this cancer that's growing in

Sermon 4 _ The Holy Spirit in Us

me," and He will! How many of you know that you can have some toxic relationships that aren't healthy for you or bad habits like gambling or drinking or gossiping or overeating? As children of the Most High God, we must give them all over to God, amen?

The last one is **omnipresent**, that is to say, that He is everywhere. He's been everywhere, and He is everywhere all at the same time. You can't say that you were in a situation that God couldn't help you with because God was over in Fairfax City helping someone else.

He is not in Centerville, only helping me. He doesn't work that way. He is everywhere, all at the same time. We are so tiny compared to Him, so it's not a big deal for Him to be everywhere.

He is **sovereign**, that is to say, He is King. A King in His Kingdom does have to ask anyone for anything because all that can be seen in His Kingdom is His. He's sovereign, and this is His role; this is His game. None of us are going to stand up and say that we don't like this arrangement and that we are going to change the rules to this. No, we're not because we aren't big enough or bad enough.

God is **truth**. Now don't get this confused. I didn't say He is true, which He is. I said that God is truth. What does that mean? That means that He cannot tell a lie. He cannot state something that is not inherently true. Every word out of God's

God's Purpose and Plan for your Life

mouth is true…it's automatically true.

God is **Holy**. We serve a Holy God. These may be things we already know, but how do we know them? We know because we look at our Bibles, and it says the Holy Bible. That's His Word. When He speaks it, not only is it true, but it is also Holy. Holy means "made for use by God." But, we are made for use by God, too, so guess what? We are holy too! Hallelujah! God is **righteous**; that is to say, God is the source of all right living. God is **Good**. He is a good God. God is omniscient, omnipotent, omnipresent, sovereign, truth, Holy, righteous, Good, and more! Knowing the character of God helps us know God.

If you have a father and you ask him for a fish, generally speaking, he wouldn't turn around and hand you a stone. Your father isn't going to do that to you because he cares about you and he provides for you, and he loves you. He is not just loving… to you, he is love. Similarly, in Romans 5:8, the apostle Paul reminds us that "God commendeth His love toward us that while we were yet sinners, Christ died for us."

Jesus came into this world and lived as a man among us. He talked about God Jehovah as our Father, and now we talk about Jesus as the Son. To a large degree, each one of us can grasp those concepts because we all have fathers, and some of us are fathers. So, we understand that concept, but here comes the third Person of the Trinity.

Sermon 4 _ The Holy Spirit in Us

Knowing the Holy Spirit

The Holy Spirit is hard to grasp. A Spirit can't be seen with the human eye, so how can we understand it? As children of God, we need to better understand the father, the Son, and the Holy Spirit. God is a triune God. Triune means three in one. It doesn't mean that we are not polytheistic serving three gods. We are monotheistic and believe in serving only one God. But how can this be? To better explain, let me provide an example.

You take a glass and fill it half full with boiling hot water right out the teapot, and then you throw some ice cubes in it. At that moment you see a triune cup of water! In that cup, you will see steam coming out the top, which is a gas, while you will see that you have water in the bottom of the cup, which is a liquid, while you will see that you have solid ice cubes floating on top of the water. Although it may exist in three different phases, it is still all water.

> At that moment you see **a triune cup of water!**

That's an example of how God is. Sometimes you'll hear the word "Trinity." Some may say that since you can't find the word "Trinity" in the Bible, then it doesn't exist. Well, the word "cell phone" doesn't appear in the Bible, and still, it exists! So, just because some word doesn't appear in the Bible doesn't mean that it doesn't exist. The concept of the Trinity is there, and you just have to look for it.

You take a look at Genesis; you don't have to go very deep into the Bible before you see the Trinity.

The word "cell phone" doesn't appear in the Bible, **and still, it exists!**

In Genesis 1: 26, we see that is the first time you hear God refer to the Trinity as "Us"; it reads, "And God said, Let us make man in our image, after our likeness." In Genesis 11:7, before the Tower of Babel, God says, "Let us go down and confused their language so that they would not be able to understand one another's speech."

Additionally, in the New Testament, in 1 John 5:7, Apostle John tells us, "For there are three that bear record in heaven, the Father, the Word, and the Holy Ghost: and these three are one." In Matthew 3:16-17, it says, "As soon as Jesus was baptized, He went up out of the water. At that moment, heaven was opened, and he saw the Spirit of God descending like a dove and alighting on Him. And a voice from heaven said, "This is my Son, whom I love; with Him I am well pleased."

Now you see there again three in one. You have the voice calling out from heaven; that is the Father. He looks down and sees Jesus and says, well done, my Son. And then you see the Holy Spirit come down in the form of a dove. This concept of triune shouldn't be that foreign to us. It really isn't all that

Sermon 4 _ The Holy Spirit in Us

deep if you think about it because each one of us is a triune being too. Remember when God said that He made us in His likeness and in his image. His likeness means that just like He is three in one, then we are also three in one, and we appear like God.

We are triune. We have a mental mind. If I tell you to close your eyes and think of a steak on the grill, pretty soon, you can hear it crackling, and you can smell the aroma. But where is that steak right now? It's nowhere but in your mind. It doesn't exist in the physical world, but you can smell it, you can hear it, and you can see it. So, you live in a mental world that is not confined to the physical limitations of the physical world.

You also live in a physical world, so if I pinch your arm, you will feel it. But you also live in a spiritual world. This means that your spirit lives, and breathes, and has its being. It needs to be fed, it needs exercise every now and then, and most importantly, it needs to be plugged into God. So, today that's what we are going to look at The Holy Spirit…God's Holy Spirit. What did He come here to do and not do?

So, while Jesus was walking on earth with the disciples, the disciples had the ability to touch Him and shake His hand. They could see all of His mannerisms and in the way He carried Himself, and they could listen to His teachings. But He came to them and said, "I will pray to the father that He shall give you another comforter." Now prior to Jesus saying those words to the disciples, there was no use of the word "comfort-

God's Purpose and Plan for your Life

er." From the Greek paracletes, comforter means "One who comes alongside and helps"; that's who our Comforter is. As a result of Jesus dying on the cross, every true believer receives the Holy Spirit on the inside—hallelujah!

The Holy Spirit comes to convict us of the sin in our lives. Does that mean that the Holy Spirit is here to pick over every sin that we do? If that were the case, He would come to convict us of our sins, plural. No. He came to convict us of sin and to remind us of the fact that we can't get to heaven on our own. The way we live is wrong in the eyes of God, so the Holy Spirit came to show us that we need Jesus in our lives.

How many of us have heard people say, "I'm wrong, but I'm not that wrong" or "I looked at the Ten Commandments, and I didn't kill anyone today?" In reality, all you have to do is commit one sin, and you are guilty of them all! You may not have killed someone, but you have told a lie or stole something that didn't belong to you or committed adultery. If you are running your mouth and gossiping, you committed sin also.

*In reality, all you have to do is commit one sin, and **you are guilty of them all!***

If you were speeding on the highway getting to church this morning, then you broke the law, which is a transgression.

Thank God for Jesus because I couldn't keep a ledger

big enough for all of my faults. Amen? But don't judge me too harshly because I'm sure you would say the same if I started to pull down this movie screen and show some of your sins, faults, iniquities, or transgressions.

Some may live in a world where they don't think that they do anything that is that bad. Jesus said if you think about a sinful act, and if you ponder it and entertain it in your mind too long, then you're guilty of sin. You are guilty of it. Now, if I pull the screen down and don't show the church all of the sins you've committed, but instead, I show them all of the thoughts that you've been thinking about, who can stand it? Touch your neighbor and say, "Thank God for Jesus!"

The Holy Spirit comes to convict us of Sin with a capital "S." He shows us that we are sinners and that we need Jesus. When we share with others how good God has been to us and how God saved us, they may say, "That's fine for you that you have been saved." But that's not enough.

That's why when we meet people, and we want to encourage them, we must also show them the wrong they may be doing. A lot of times, we show them only the good times, emphasizing "come to my church," Jesus is not even mentioned. They don't need to come to our church; what they really need is to find Jesus Christ and be saved! They need to hear from us what Jesus has done for us.

Whether they end up coming to Tree of Life Bible Church

or not is irrelevant. Although I'd love to see this church packed out, the reality is that God may not be leading that person to our church. God only asked us to sow the seed. Although sowing the seed requires us to remind them that they are a sinner, they might not like that. They might look at you like you're an idiot, but the reality is that's what we are called here to do. We are called to be different.

We are to be salt. Have you ever noticed that when you put salt on foods, you can taste the food better? You are meant to be salty. You are meant to stand out. God needs us to rise up and be what we were called to be.

You are meant to **stand out.**

The Holy Spirit came to bring us to Jesus. John 16:3 says, "These things will they do unto you because they have not known the Father nor me." So, the Holy Spirit brings us to a knowledge of Jesus. Verse 13 takes us even further and says, "howbeit when the spirit of truth is come, He will guide you into all truth. for He shall not speak of Himself, but whatsoever He shall hear that what He shall speak, and He will show you all things to come."

So, The Holy Spirit has come to give us all truth. To guide us and direct us. The Holy Spirit came to show you your need for righteousness because we need to live a righteous life, and sometimes, we skip over that. You shouldn't get saved and then do whatever you want to do. Righteousness is right living, but how can you live right if you don't study your Word? Do you have the Daily Bible Reading for this year? If so, then you should be studying your Word daily.

Matthew 5:20 says, "For I say unto you, That except your righteousness shall exceed the righteousness of the scribes and Pharisees, ye shall in no case enter into the kingdom of heaven." The reality is, it's not that we want to compare ourselves to Pharisees because your righteousness is not false righteousness, and it is not based on self-righteousness, but it is based upon the righteousness of Jesus.

If you think you are going to make it into heaven for your own goodness' sake, that's wrong thinking. You won't make it in. So that self-righteousness is going to get you zero because we can't get into heaven based upon our own intrinsic goodness. We've got to get to heaven based on faith in Jesus Christ. And we won't get to heaven if we don't get saved.

> If you think you are going to make it into heaven for your own goodness' sake, **that's wrong thinking. You won't make it.**

And we might not stay close to God if we don't keep ourselves in His Word. **First**, the Holy Spirit has come to convict us of our Sin. **Second**, the Holy Spirit comes to bring us to Jesus.

Third, the Holy Spirit comes to show us our need for righteousness. **Fourth**, the Holy Spirit did not come to be lied to. There's a story in Acts 5:1-10, about a man named Ananias and his wife Sapphira who lied to the Holy Spirit, and it begins, "But a certain man named Ananias, with Sapphira, his wife, sold a possession. And he kept back part of the proceeds, his wife also being aware of it, and brought a certain part and laid it at the apostles' feet. But Peter said, "Ananias, why has Satan filled your heart to lie to the Holy Spirit and keep back part of the price of the land for yourself? While it remained, was it not your own? And after it was sold, was it not in your own control? Why have you conceived this thing in your heart? You have not lied to men but to God."

You have to really break this story apart to get the meaning. There was a piece of land that they sold, and if they wanted to, then they could have kept all of the money from the sale. There was no requirement that they had to give the money. These were two people who probably prayed to God to get this land in the first place! They got the price that they asked for, and maybe even more. Then, they promised the Lord that they would give Him all of it. They did not have to make that promise to God, but they did. Now when the time came, instead of giving all of it to the Lord, they chose to keep some of it, and they laid the rest of it at the apostles' feet.

It's like not only do I want to give this money, but I want fame. I'm going to go to Vatican City and lay it at the Pope's feet. I want the whole world to see that I gave all of my money to God, while actually, I want to keep some of it back. Who did they think they were fooling? Didn't I preach on omniscient as being one of the characteristics of God? God knew it all, so it made no sense for this couple to lie to God or to try and fool the apostles.

So, fast forward, and the husband, Ananias, drops dead right where he stood and in the middle of his sentence. Now, the disciples carry him out, and the wife comes in. You would think right then and there. She would want to change her story. The apostles asked her, "What happened, Sapphira?" But she started lying too, just like her husband and then all of a sudden, she died! The Holy Spirit did not come to be lied to.

The number one thing that is disliked within the church is hypocrisy within church folk. They may think to themselves, "You talk all of that church stuff, but I see the real you at work," "I see how you come late to work, how you leave early, how you take two-hour lunches, and how you take office supplies home," "I know everything you are doing, and you call yourself saved, a Christian, and a child of God," and "after all of that you want me to follow you?" To what?

Fifth, the Holy Spirit did not come to be grieved. Did you know that you could grieve the Holy Spirit? In Ephesians 4:29-32, it tells us, "Let no corrupt word proceed out of your mouth, but what is good for necessary edification, that it may impart grace to the hearers. And do not grieve the Holy Spirit of God,

God's Purpose and Plan for your Life

by whom you were sealed for the day of redemption. Let all bitterness, wrath, anger, clamor, and evil speaking be put away from you, with all malice. And be kind to one another, tenderhearted, forgiving one another, even as God in Christ forgave you."

So, how we act and how we treat one another in the world can make the Holy Spirit happy or can grieve the Holy Spirit. What does grieve mean? Grieve means causing sadness and sorrowfulness. What makes the Holy Spirit sad? Foul, bitter, obscene, profane, and vulgar language, dirty jokes, and scandalous gossip. Whenever we are texting one another, how much of it is made up of this type of language?

What about Facebook? Granted, I don't fully understand Facebook to the point where I have deleted my account twice because I just don't get it. I understand texting, but Facebook I just don't understand. But one thing I have learned about it is that for many church members, there is a different you on Facebook. Just remember that foul communication grieves the Holy Spirit. It grieves Him because He is saying, I know I saved them, so why are they acting this way. I know that we all just want to fit in, but remember, God wants us to be salt!

In both Matthew 12 and Luke 6, Jesus talks and says, "Out of the abundance of the heart the mouth speaks." So, what you put on Facebook is coming from your heart. You are one way at school, you are another way at church, you're acting another way on Facebook, and that shouldn't be the case.

Sermon 4 _ The Holy Spirit in Us

The Bible tells us that the heart of man is desperately wicked. When you post pictures on the Internet, you can never get them back, even when you delete them. You think you've deleted them, but they're still there. There are cached copies, and there are backed-up copies.

If you ever become famous, guess what pictures are coming out? In 1 Corinthians 15:33, Paul tells us, "Be not deceived, evil communication corrupts good manners." This scripture is saying that even though it might just be evil words, then pretty soon, it will turn into evil manners. So, when you start acting hoochie on Facebook, you will start acting hoochie in the real world.

Did you hear about senator Gifford's who was shot in the head outside of a Safeway grocery store? In that situation, they showed on 60 Minutes how the shooter went from being a regular guy to a deranged guy to a murderer. And it turns out that it was all done in little baby steps. It started out with him talking about some things, and then he began to get exposed to some writings from other people, then he started getting interested in politics and guns, then he actually went out and bought a gun, then he took pictures with his gun and put it on Facebook.

Do you get the connection so far? What you do in this virtual world starts to bleed out in the real world.

Are we looking at some pornography on the Internet?

When you look lustfully at a woman, then you've already slept with her. It's time to clean up our act. **Sixth**, the Holy Spirit did not come to be quenched. First Thessalonians 5:19 says, "quench not the spirit." That's all it says! Quenching is like pouring a bucket of water out and putting out a fire. Do you remember what pastor used to say? He said each of us could carry a bucket of gasoline or a bucket of water with us. For someone who just got saved and is on fire for the Lord, they may be so on fire for the Lord and excited, but they might say a few things that may not be 100 percent scriptural because they are still learning. But they love the Lord.

And here you come with your bucket of water telling, "I'm sorry to do that, but you used the wrong word in the wrong scripture." By saying that, you just poured a bucket of water on their little flame! That's the word "quench." Paul used the word "quench" because it doesn't mean that something is on fire, so you took just a little water to put it out. You are not sure if it might be out, or it might not. No, quench means you're going to make sure it's out. That's the word he used when he's talking about the Holy Spirit.

You may say that you don't quench the Holy Spirit. But, how many times has there been an altar call, and you feel the urging of the Holy Spirit pulling you to go up to the altar, but you say, "Nope, that's not for me?" The pastor might even be calling you out by name, and still, you resist. That's quenching the Spirit. You are dousing out the urging of the Holy Spirit. Or,

Sermon 4 _ The Holy Spirit in Us

that urging that God puts inside of you is there to draw you to speak to someone who needs to hear the Word of God.

If you stop it or dismiss it, then you are quenching the Spirit. Maybe you have a situation to where something is not good in your life going on. This isn't the Holy Spirit urging you to do something. It is the Holy Spirit urging you to stop doing something. You know you're not supposed to be doing that; perhaps it could be a sexual situation.

The Holy Spirit is trying to draw you out of that mess because He knows where it's eventually going to take you. He is God, and He sees the future, and He knows where this is going to take you. If this sounds like you, then today, stop quenching the spirit when God is trying to tell you something, and you are too busy texting or talking to someone. He is trying to stop you from going off a cliff.

The altar is open this morning, and once again, Jesus is calling someone. If you want Jesus to come into your heart today, then come! If you have backslidden and otherwise feel disconnected from God, then come! If you want to come and stand in the gap for a family member or close friend, then now is your time to come!

Today, we talked about what the Holy Spirit came to do and not do, so let me ask you today, as you are thinking back over your life, are you resisting the urging of the Holy Spirit in your life? Do you know in your heart that God is talking to

God's Purpose and Plan for your Life

you through the Holy Spirit, perhaps urging you to speak to someone and you're holding back? The Holy Spirit may be speaking to you right now about a certain sin within a certain area of your life, and you may be deliberately shutting out the Holy Spirit.

You may feel like you are a hypocrite because you act a certain way on Sunday morning but act differently throughout the week. We can fool all the people some of the time, and we can fool some people all of the time. But we can't fool God any of the time!

> We can fool all the people some of the time, and we can fool some people all of the time. But **we can't fool God any of the time!**

Sermon 5 – Jesus, Our Lord, Makes Us New All Over

Verses: 2 Corinthians 5:17
(Originally preached on November 28, 2010)

"Therefore, if any man be in Christ, he is a new creature: old things are passed away; behold, all things are become new."

2 Corinthians 5:17, KJV

Praise the Lord, church. Praise the Lord, church! We start off this life in a natural state of sin. If you ever notice the little kids as they run around here. You will notice that even though they are young, you don't have to teach them to tell a lie. You have to teach them pretty much everything else, like how to sit, talk, walk, poop, eat, and drink, but you don't have to teach them how to tell a lie.

The Old Man

They may say to their mothers, "No, mommy, I didn't eat the cookies," but their mother can see all of the cookie crumbs that are all around their mouths. How did they get that good at

Sermon 5 – *Jesus, Our Lord, Makes Us New All Over*

lying? It's because it is our natural state. Our natural state is to be sinful and to be lost.

Thank God, however, that He has put in us a natural inclination to find our way back to Him out of this lost state. There is something that pulls us. I'm so thankful for everyone that is here. This is not a message for someone coming in off the street, but instead, today's message is for born-again believers only. Today's message is entitled "Jesus Our Lord Makes Us New All Over."

Oftentimes you might think to yourself, "I pretty much have me figured out." But living in this world, sometimes someone messes with us, and some of them even get on our nerves. Some of them make us want to take our religion off and put it up on a shelf, making us think to ourselves, "Lord, you go sit up here on a shelf while I'll go take care of my business, and then I'll come back and put you back on later." I guess I'm not the only one that may have thought that.

What we are really dealing with is a battle that's going on inside of us for control of us. When you first get saved, Jesus comes into your heart. He has now taken possession, ownership, or at least residence in our hearts. We might let Him in and yet not let Him have control. Now you have this battle going on. We are living in the flesh, seeking what pleases us and us alone, lost, and we actually lose our capacity to seek out God because we are lost and sinful.

But, thank God, when Jesus came into our lives, and now, we can please God, because as the Bible teaches us, without faith, you can't please God. You'll never be able to. Here is probably the second best verse in the whole Bible, 2 Corinthians 5:17. If you memorized any verses in the Bible, the first verse would probably be John 3:16. Everyone knows that one, even if you don't go to a church.

If you go to a professional NFL football game, you might even see John 3:16 on a big poster. So, the second verse you should memorize is this scripture right here...2 Corinthians 5:17, and it reads, "Therefore if any man be in Christ, he or she is a new creature. Old things are passed away. Behold, all things become new."

New Creatures in Christ

Let's think about this now. We knew that we were new creatures, but what does that mean? You know what it is to be the old creature, old man, or old woman because that's what you came into this world with. You came into this world with eyes, hands, and a heart that beats.

So, if you know what the old you is like, you can start getting your mind wrapped around what your new you would be like. You have two new spiritual eyes, being able to see the world God's way. You have a new tender heart, replacing the old stony heart. You have a new mind if you have let God

Sermon 5 – *Jesus, Our Lord, Makes Us New All Over*

change it. The Bible tells us, "Let this mind be in you." It says **let**, and it doesn't say God will **make** you have this mind.

Today's topic is that Jesus Our Lord makes us new all over, and this is going to set the tone for something called the Baptism of the Spirit. But it's going to take me a while to get there, so you have to be patient with me. First, we start in a lost state that is our natural state, and we cannot get to heaven without a change happening. What scripture is that change found in? First Corinthians 5:17 and Ephesians 2:3, wherein the apostle Paul tells us, "Among whom also we all had our conversation in times past in the lusts of our flesh, fulfilling the desires of the flesh and of the mind; and were by nature the children of wrath, even as others."

Who calls us the children of wrath? Paul does. This was when we were out there in the world, and we thought we had everything figured out, and we thought that we weren't that bad, but Paul calls you the children of wrath, saying, "Knowing this, that our old man was crucified with Him, that the body of sin might be done away with, that we should no longer be slaves of sin."

So, we see that in our old nature, our old man, or our old woman, we are called the children of wrath. But now, as the new man and the new woman of God, we are described by our capacity for sharing the good news of the gospel of Jesus Christ. And we are described as our capacity of glorifying God instead of ourselves. And by our capacity to serve God in righteousness.

Think about it, when you were in the world, was your mind focused on any of those things? Maybe you have been born again and saved all of your life, but I wasn't. I grew up in the church, but how many of you know that you can grow up in the church and still be a sinner? Straight up sinning? You can be a straight-up sinner and still be going to church.

We're not really talking about church this morning, are we? We aren't even talking about holding a position in the church. We're talking about being saved, sanctified, Holy Ghost-filled, and fire baptized! So, now that we have been given a made-up mind and we have a changed heart, we are now new creatures.

A New Mind

Let's take a look at some of these things. First, a changed mind. We get wrapped up in a lot of words in the Bible that, if we are not careful, can trip us up. You'll see a word in the Bible, and you have to understand it's been translated time and time again. And through these translations, you can lose the meaning. Have you ever played that game at school when you were a kid where everyone sat in a circle, and you whispered a secret story in the ear of the person next to you, and it goes around until you get to the last person? If so, then you know that by the time it comes back to you, it's a totally differ-

Sermon 5 – *Jesus, Our Lord, Makes Us New All Over*

ent story.

Some of these words can lose their essence if you don't take the time to really dig them out and research their meaning. So, the word "mind" is translated as "attitude." What's the number one thing that parents are fussing at their kids about these days? Their attitude! Every time you hear "mind," replace it with "attitude," so "let this attitude be in you that was also in Christ Jesus." And what attitude did Jesus have?

When Jesus spoke, He didn't always answer people based upon what was asked of Him, but His answer was targeted to exactly what their heart needed to hear. When Jesus is listening to you, He is not listening to the words that come from your lips. Instead, He is listening to your heart.

We need to get the attitude of Christ. How do we get the attitude of Christ? As we have seen earlier, when dealing with the issue of your attitude, you are dealing with the issue of your mind. Change your attitude, and therefore, you will change your mind. With Salvation comes a new word, regeneration. Think about that, though. First, you generate something, and then you regenerate it.

Change your attitude, and therefore, you will **change your mind.**

So, something had to have been generated the first time for it to generate again, amen? If you were born into this world as a physical human baby, you were "generated."

Now comes a second time through salvation, and you're "regenerated." That means you get a regenerated mind, and you get a regenerated attitude! You can't sit back and say, "I've been saved, sanctified, Holy Ghost-filled, and fire-baptized, but my attitude is exactly what it was when you met me ten years ago." I may agree with you on a lot of things, but I can't agree with that! If you have been saved, then you have been changed, but if you have not been changed, how do you know you have been saved?

My name is signed in heaven like the song says, "the angels in Heaven just signed my name." But, if true, shouldn't others see a change for the better in us? If you are still the same attitudinal person you've always been, then perhaps you need to check yourself. If you are not sure, perhaps even ask your friends about your attitude. Just don't get your lip poked out when they tell you their answer.

Philippians 2:5 tells us, "Let this mind be in you which was also in Christ Jesus." We have to have a new mind and a new attitude, but how is it renewed? It is renewed with Christ's mind and Christ's attitude. Our new mind means having a new, more positive attitude towards others and having a new outlook on life. That means whenever I'm interacting with you, am I seeing you with my earthly eyes, or do I see you through Christ's eyes?

Sermon 5 – *Jesus, Our Lord, Makes Us New All Over*

Do I greet you as Christ would greet you? We should see the face of Jesus in the face of each other. Remember, the old you is still inside of you, and anyone who tells you otherwise is lying. When Jesus comes into your heart, He puts the old you in a box, He closes and seals the lid, and then He sits on that lid. The old man can't come out unless you tell Jesus to get off that lid to let him out for a little while as you handle things on your own, and then Jesus will let him come out. But it's your choice.

God did not make us robots, but instead, He gave us free will. So, we have to get a change in our mind and a change in our attitude. If someone treats you wrong, the new man would say like Jesus in Luke 23:34, "Father, forgive them; for they know not what they do." Jesus got all kind of mistreated, and yet on His worst day, He saw fit to forgive people. So, let's have that mindset of forgiving one another. Why? Because you have Jesus living inside of you now.

Someone lies on you at work or at school, and you bust them in that lie. How are we going to respond? We could say, "You hurt me, and so now I'm going to hurt you back." Or we can do like Jesus in John 8:11 and say, "Neither do I condemn thee: go, and sin no more." What would that do to a person? They would be like, "I have to find out what's going on with this guy because he is different than most people." Isn't that what we are supposed to be portraying? While we are on this earth aren't, we supposed to emulate Christ. The precepts of forgiveness instead of condemnation that Christ taught won't live again unless they live through us.

> The precepts of forgiveness instead of condemnation that Christ taught won't live again **unless they live through us.**

Whatever it was that drew you into a loving and saving relationship with Christ, we all need to think back to what it was. See, the funny thing about God is that He reaches each one of us through someone else. Each person you can think of was brought here by someone else. What was it about that person that brought you here? There was always a physical person that touched you in a way and reached into your heart to make you see that "you know that there is a God who loves you!"

Are you living that life today so that someone else can believe in Jesus through you? You are not going to reach anyone if you don't get a changed mind or a changed attitude. Our new attitude can prevent us from thinking too highly of ourselves. Our new attitude will cultivate a mind like Christ's. Our new attitude will seek humility rather than pride. Today's age is all about being proud of what you can do, where you have gone, and all about your accomplishments. But pride can take you too far to where pretty soon, you don't care about anyone else.

What was the first sin ever done in the whole existence of

Sermon 5 – *Jesus, Our Lord, Makes Us New All Over*

time? Pride! Even before mankind showed up on the scene, Satan rose up and said, "I'm better than the other angels, and I'm equal with God." When you rise up and say you are better than someone else, you are not really diminishing them, but instead, you are diminishing their creator.

Christ's new attitude will start to get us to submit ourselves to the will of God and to understand the example of Jesus Christ. Are we known for speaking our mind? Are we known for blaming others when they misunderstand? Have you heard the phrase "s/he doesn't suffer fools lightly?" If so, that means if you did something wrong, then that person will be really quick to correct you or get you told. Is that the way we're supposed to be?

When we rise up like that, we are actually rising up against the creator. Instead, we need to be patient with one another. We need to be sensitive with one another. This is not a message for someone coming in the door that has never known Jesus. This is a message for us saved and sanctified individuals. There are those in the world that want to hurt us and break our hearts. And sometimes, the very people you think are the closest to you are the ones that will set you up and break your heart.

That's why the apostle Peter, in 1 Peter 1:13, tells us to "Wherefore gird up the loins of your mind, be sober, and hope to the end for the grace that is to be brought unto you at the revelation of Jesus Christ." So, Peter is telling us to protect our attitude. How do you protect your attitude? Well, it starts with what you are feeding it and what you take in.

We need to have a controlled attitude. Our controlled attitude will protect us from loose and undisciplined thoughts. Because what's happening up here in the mind sooner or later will come out there in the heart. Right now, we are living in an epidemic of online pornography. That's a dirty word that no one talks about anymore, yet news sources have reported that pornography is even an epidemic in the church!

The Temptations of this World

When you take a look at the statistics, you're looking at three out of ten church-goers who have looked at pornography. It may be increasing due to the ease and availability of free online Internet pornography, but still, that's a lot of people in the church that are struggling with sex and lust. We have to start by not having loose and undisciplined thoughts. Because those thoughts that we entertain sooner or later will come out. Hurt people hurt people.

If you are hurting inside, then you are just a ticking time bomb ready to go off, but remember that if you

Hurt people **hurt people.**

are hurt, then you are in the right place. You came to the spiritual hospital, and Jesus is going to fix you up. Keep in mind

Sermon 5 – *Jesus, Our Lord, Makes Us New All Over*

that you have the potential of hurting the very people that love you in this church. If brother Calvin hurts my feelings, I have to have enough love in my heart to say to myself, "I know brother Calvin didn't really mean it; he is just hurting right now."

Sometimes hurt people just want to talk and vent, and they just need someone to listen. Sometimes we have to rise up bigger than our own egos, reminding ourselves that this thing is bigger than little old me. I need to love them through their situation or their irresponsible action.

Sometimes when your mind is not right, you will go out and do the strangest stuff. A woman told me once that she was always attracted to the wrong men. I told her to turn around, go the other way, and not continue doing the same thing while expecting different outcomes. What about people who are alcoholics and who were trying to get off the booze, but they hang out at the bar. That's crazy, right? Or, people who try to lose weight, but they're eating every day at the fast-food restaurant.

Paul, in Romans 12:1-2, tells us, "I beseech you therefore, brethren, by the mercies of God, that ye present your bodies a living sacrifice, holy, acceptable unto God, which is your reasonable service. And be not conformed to this world: but be ye transformed by the renewing of your mind, that ye may prove what is that good, and acceptable, and perfect, will of God."

In the movie called *Transformers*, a VW bug changes into

a robot, and then, later on, another transformer changes from a boom box, and it turns into a robot. There is a transformer that is a jet that turns into a robot. They all end up turning into different types of robots. They've transformed from one state to another state.

That's what Paul is saying here. Your mind needs transformation. It needs to change from what it was born to be and into now what it needs to become, through the power of the saving blood of Jesus! Remember that with salvation comes that "r" word, regeneration. Through regeneration, Jesus gives us a regenerated mind and a regenerated attitude.

I want to give an example. What happens at the Turkey bowl on Thursday? Sister Latoya had her cheerleading squad ready. Not only did all of the cheerleaders know their cheers, but they all also had on cute matching cheerleader outfits. They arrived professionally, and they even provided everyone with a little halftime program.

It just so happens that the other side of the field wasn't as organized or prepared. There could have been some feelings of jealousy, but what ended up happening was that some of the young ladies on the other side of the field began hollering across the field, and then three of them eventually came over to our side of the field.

It's an honor to the leader when the followers behave right. I don't know if all of our cheerleaders realized this, but

Sermon 5 – *Jesus, Our Lord, Makes Us New All Over*

they honored Latoya when they behaved themselves well. You didn't see cheerleaders pulling off the earrings, you didn't see any high heels come off, and no fighting. We were all very proud of the way our church handled ourselves.

A New Heart

Next, we need to have a change in our hearts. You have to have a changed heart to have a changed mind. The heart is the seat of your emotions. Into your heart flows all the inputs of your five senses, and out of the well of the heart flows rejoicing, sorrow, and desires. So, regeneration from Salvation needs to give us a new heart, as well. So, you may start off with your old heart that cared only about you.

> The heart is the **seat of your emotions.**

The new heart now starts to care about other people. It says in God's Word that "the one that loved the most is the one that was given the most." It amazes you when you start to realize how bad you were and how far from heaven you were and how close to hell you were and how Jesus swooped down and grabbed you up at the last second!

Paul, in Romans 10:10, tells us, "For with the heart man believeth unto righteousness; and with the mouth, confession is made unto salvation." The writer of the book of Hebrews, in Hebrews 3:8, warns us as Christians that if we are not careful, our hearts can become hardened. We are told that to protect our hearts from that hardness; we need to encourage other Christians in fellowship. Our hearts start out in this world as what the Bible calls them "desperately wicked."

Next, we need to study God's Word. And I always hit on this in every one of my sermons. I emphasize studying your Word and not simply rushing through your reading of His Word, like scanning the morning newspaper. Study your Word each day because 99 percent of the problems that are in our lives and what we're dealing with can be traced back to us not studying our Word. We need to get our hearts changed.

Be less hard to ourselves and others. It is our job to protect our heart from the lust and the temptations of the flesh, the world, and the devil. There are things that are hitting at our heart, like if you watch too much TV or you watch too much news, they can wear on your heart. Do you feel like you have a new heart?

You can't tell me at the end of this sermon, "thank you for telling me what you told me, but my heart hasn't changed." Remember, you are not saved if you have not been regenerated. While we have this walk with the Lord, we all have to realize that we are all at different levels, and we are all at different stages, so we all have to be patient with one another.

Sermon 5 – Jesus, Our Lord, Makes Us New All Over

A New Spirit

We also need a change in our spirit. Remember, this is all in preparation for the Baptism of the Spirit. Now we're going to talk about changing the spirit. Isn't it interesting that God oftentimes does things in threes? Like the Bible tells us in Ecclesiastes 4:12, "A threefold cord is not quickly broken." There were three wisemen. There is the Father, the Son, and the Holy Spirit. There is the spirit, the water, and the blood. They all come in threes.

We have a situation in our life where we, too, are three. There is the physical man, the mental man, and the spiritual man. Has there been a real and genuine change in your spirit?

That's a hard one to answer. Sometimes we have been changed, but the devil is whispering in our ear, "You know that you're not really changed." You want to reply, "Get thee behind me, Satan, because I know I've been changed." And how do we know that we are saved...because the Bible tells us so. The word of God tells us. If you don't know nothing else, you know Romans 10:8-10, which tells us that we are saved!

How do we know that we are saved...because **the Bible tells us so**.

Now that we know we're saved, do we have to have a new spirit? God gave us our spirit even before birth, so do we need it changed? Our spirit has the capacity to love at one moment and hate the next, yet the Bible says, "can a fountain give off bitter water and sweet water?"

I like the part of the Bible that teaches us that we will know a tree by the fruit it bears. You are never going to get apples from a lemon tree. Our spirit has the capacity to live truthfully one moment and live a lie the next moment, but still, how many people can say I lived a lie? We no longer need to live a defeated life that is controlled by sin because our spirit is governed by free will, which is a gift from God.

We were given an awesome gift from Christ, who paid for all of our sins. He broke the endless cycle of sin in our lives. Now, does that mean that you won't sin or that you are sin-free for the rest of your life? You know that you might still mess up, but the difference is that you are no longer comfortable with that sin and that mess. If you are saved by the grace of Jesus Christ, you will want to come up out of the sins that you've been doing.

When you give your sins to God, He tells us in Psalm 103:12, "As far as the east is from the west, so far hath He removed our transgressions from us." This morning, as you look over your life, if you messed up, it's okay you messed up. But if you took it to God, then God blessed you because He has already forgiven you and forgotten all about it.

Now my question to you is what do you do the next day? What will you do tomorrow? Now that you have been forgiv-

Sermon 5 – *Jesus, Our Lord, Makes Us New All Over*

en and given a clean slate, what do we do? We have to stop living a defeated life, and we have to start living a victorious life. We are champions! So, God breaks that cycle so that we no longer enjoy sin.

> We have to stop living a defeated life, and **we have to start living a victorious life.**

Maybe while we were out there in the world, we were sinning and didn't mind it. But, remember what I said earlier that the things that God does often comes in threes. We have to have a singleness of mind, a singleness of heart, and a singleness of spirit. Remember, singleness of mind is singleness of attitude. Think about what God has given to us.

What did He do for our minds when we got saved? What He is telling us is that if we let Him, He will come in and change our mind and our attitude, and He will make your life so much happier after Salvation than before.

What did He do for our hearts? He says in His Word that He will take away your stony heart to give you a heart that's tender for Him. If we mess up, we want to get right with the Lord, so we want to have a tender heart so that we don't get too comfortable with sin.

How about when you don't come to church? Maybe in

122

the past, you were comfortable doing that, but now you don't sit at home on a Sunday and feel comfortable not being at church. When it's Sunday, you want to be in service for the Lord, amen?

What does He do for your spirit? He says I'm going to give you my own spirit. What more can you ask for from Him? He actually puts inside of you a piece of Himself. So, now whatever you get yourself into, you are taking God with you into it. There's a part in the Bible that says if you have a mind to want to sleep with somebody, don't do that because when you enter that bed with that man or that woman, you are taking Jesus with you.

When you go and commit that sin, Jesus is right there with you. So, how does He find you? He finds you because a piece of Him is living within you. He abides in you because God gave us His only Son. God gave us salvation, regeneration, and the Baptism of the Holy Spirit so that now we are filled with the Spirit, and we are now living victorious lives.

When you go and commit that sin, Jesus is right there with you.

The Baptism of the Holy Spirit

Sermon 5 – *Jesus, Our Lord, Makes Us New All Over*

Even if you backslide or mess up now and again, that doesn't change your state because you are still victorious. You may be temporarily knocked down, but you'll get back up. Paul, in 1 Corinthians 12:13, tells us, "For by one Spirit are we all baptized into one body, whether we be Jews or Gentiles, whether we be bond or free; and have been all made to drink into one Spirit." Do you feel more victorious from last year?

Do you feel that you're growing, understanding godly wisdom, learning new godly precepts, and applying them in your life? We can say in our hearts, "I might not be the best, but I know I've come a long way from where I used to be; I'm not perfect, but I'm growing, and that's what God has called me to do."

So, let's unite with Christ through his crucifixion as Lord over our lives. That means separation from the dominion of Sin over our lives. Realize as our life is going down the road, we are passing from being interested in the world to be interested in the Lord. Look what God has done. God has transformed our minds, and God has changed our direction and attention!

> We are passing from being interested in the world to be **interested in the Lord.**

In closing, in Romans 6:4, Paul encourages us with "Therefore we are buried with Him by baptism into death: that like as Christ was raised up from the dead by the glory of the Father, even so, we also should walk in newness of life." You should have a new life, and you should walk like you have new life, because you are champions!

No matter how much we want to, we cannot save ourselves, and we can't change ourselves. You'll never be able to clean up your messes by yourself. You need Jesus to clean it up. We need to grab hold of the power of Jesus to break that sin over our lives. We must be baptized into the spirit—praise God!

Sermon 6 – Loving Christ and Keeping His Commandments

Verses: John 14:15
(Originally preached on June 27, 2004)

"If ye love me, keep my commandments."

John 14:15, KJV

I don't know if you heard this one before. Some children were making a sandwich. They had the jar of mayonnaise, bologna, cheese, lettuce, and tomato. You know how little kids can be, so when they get done making their sandwiches, they aren't really thinking of putting the remaining food away, and instead, their minds are off to the next thing. So, they left a lot of things still on the counter. A fly came by and landed on the knife.

The knife had a lot of bologna still stuck to it, so the fly started eating the bologna. The fly ended up eating all of the bologna from the tip of the knife all the way to the handle. When he gets to the handle, he is so weighted down that he falls off and hits the counter…splat! What's the moral of the story? The moral of the story is, don't jump off the handle

Sermon 6 – Loving Christ and Keeping His Commandments

when you are full of bologna! Just a little humor to start our morning! Now, let's seek God as He reveals His divine understanding to us today.

Turn your Bibles to John 14, verse 15. In it, Jesus declares, "If ye love me, keep my commandments."

What Grad Would God Give Us

We need to ask ourselves where do we feel we stand in the Lord. Just as children came out of school and received their final grades for the year, the question is what final grade will we get from the Lord? The school system has what they call interims that give you an indication of how your child is doing. If your child gets a D, then the interim score is letting you know, so that it is not a surprise and so you can get your child additional help. As a parent, you still have plenty of time to go and work with getting that child's grades up.

It's the same thing here tonight. Tonight's message is entitled "Loving Christ and Keeping His Commandments," therefore, what we are going to look at is how we are doing as Christians before God has to give us our final grade. Tonight is the night for our Christian interims.

If I gave my testimony, I would testify about how good God is, recently in light of a conversation I had with Sister Christine. She talked to me about how blessed I am saying, "There are times where God is blessing you so much so that you don't

God's Purpose and Plan for your Life

even notice all of the blessings you're getting, until someone else pulls your coat tails and says, "Let me just show you how good God is being to you." " She started to reveal to me that sometimes people don't even know how much of a blessing they are to you, and this has been such a blessing to me spiritually and to my family!

That's why testimonies are so important. So, when the opportunity to testify comes to us, let's give our testimony on how good God has been in our lives. Had I realized how much of a blessing it was for me to meet someone who is a one-in-a-billion woman like my wife, Minnie? To meet her, to fall in love with her, and then to marry her was such a blessing! And then, what would be the odds that someway, somehow God would bless me to meet another one-in-a-billion person?

> How much of a blessing it was for me to meet someone who is a one-in-a-billion woman like **my wife, Minnie?**

When people think of Minnie and me, they will think that I went out to look for this one-in-a-billion person, but In reality, God presented her to me, and I thank God for that. That would be my testimony; that I'm in love and when you are in love, you can't think about anything else, you can't sleep, and you can't eat!

Sermon 6 – *Loving Christ and Keeping His Commandments*

Falling in Love with God

When you are in love, you always want to be near that person. You can't seem to do enough for them, and they are always doing more and more for you. You can't wait for the wedding day to come, and waiting for that day to come feels like it's going to take forever. As Christians, we need to realize that Christ loves us that way, and we need to love Him back that much.

Let us not be hypocritical Christians. Let's not say one thing and do another. Let us not attribute to someone things that they shouldn't do, while at the same time we are doing them. King Solomon tells us in Proverbs 7:1-3, "My son, keep my words, and lay up my commandments with thee. Keep my commandments, and live; and my law as the apple of thine eye. Bind them upon thy fingers, write them upon the table of thine heart."

When we get to heaven, there will be no husbands and wives, but we will all be children of God. So, when it says my son, it is talking about all of us. Proverbs was written from a father to his son, which is a spiritual relationship as well. So, this is to all of us. It starts with "keep my words." When I looked up the word "keep," it had several meanings, including "holding on to something and clinging to it as precious, not wanting to lose it."

Like that song we sing, "hold on to God's unchanging

hand!" Whenever we hold on to God's hand, we don't do it haphazardly or lightly because His hand is clinging to us too! It also means "retaining something, owning it, maintaining it like keeping up a property," or even storing up like "treasures in heaven."

Like that song we sing, "**hold on to God's unchanging hand!**"

In actuality, the Lord's use of these words is the same. It can be seen in each way. So, when Solomon is bringing us these words, they can be seen to have application for each of us. So, what are we to keep? We are to keep God's laws, His commandments, and His words to the best of our ability and to bind them on our fingers.

Verse 3 says, "bind them upon thy fingers and write them on the table of thine heart." This means to keep it as the apple of your eye; it means you keep it at the forefront of your mind, and it means that you are constantly caring for it. That's how we are to hold onto God's Word. We are not supposed to learn something new from God and then not give it any credence nor really value it. After the service, if I were to ask some of you, "what were some of the things that I talked about today," a few of you might say, "I don't know. I kind of remember some of it, but not all of it."

As God's ministers, we are responsible for the teaching that God gives to us. When I stand here before you, I

Sermon 6 – Loving Christ and Keeping His Commandments

As God's ministers, we are responsible for **the teaching that God gives to us.**

am standing here as the mouthpiece for God. I am God's mouthpiece to you. This is the Word of God that you are getting right now. God is bringing you His own Word today. Now, how responsible are we for keeping God's Word?

Valuing God's Word Shows Love

Brother Rob valued God's Word, and he jumped up and said he had to get a pen and paper to write down the scriptures being preached. That's valuing God's Word. It's important to God that we keep His Word. So, bind them on your fingers and write them on the table of your heart.

It's important to God that we **keep His Word.**

Similarly, Solomon tells us in Proverbs 3:3, "Let not mercy and truth forsake thee: bind them about thy neck; write them upon the table of thine heart." Again, we see that studying and committing to memory God's Word is important because these are heavenly gifts of mercy and truth. We see that there is more in this scripture, but we have to work our way backwards, so let's go to verse 1. It reads, "My son, forget not my law; but let thine heart keep my commandments: For length of days, and long life, and peace, shall they add to thee."

From this, you see that there are benefits that come from keeping God's Word. If you want to live a long life, then keep God's Word. Remember when you were a child, say, seven years old, and the days seemed to last forever, but now that you are much older, each day just seems to be whipping by. Time seems to go by so fast that you think to yourself, "is it the end of the year already? Where did the time go?"

Reading verse 3 a little closer, we see that not only will you get life, but also "length of days." Each day will be longer, but only if you keep God's commandments. So, how do we keep God's commandments? How do we keep God's Word? It first involves divine hearing.

Good sound gospel preaching is now available on TV, on the radio, and on the Internet in every country in the world. If Christian media producers were to get a report card for spreading the gospel message throughout the world, then they would get an A, or they would get an A+ for this. As the Bible tells us in Romans 10:14, "how shall they hear without a preacher?"

I read a report this week that in one Evangelistic effort in India that the good gospel message was preached to over 30,000,000 people at one time! It also said that this was not a one-time thing but was now available to people all over India.

Sermon 6 – Loving Christ and Keeping His Commandments

The gospel message is now being preached in their own language and being taught by their own people.

The interesting thing about the country of India is that it is a country of Buddhism and Hinduism. It is called the land of a million gods because over there, everything is a god. The chair you are sitting on is a god. The shirt you wear is a god. The comb you used to comb your hair, too, that's god. They believe that you have to treat all of these articles in an elevated, deified way because in their minds, they are all gods.

This reminds you of the apostle Paul, in Acts 17:23, where he recounts entering into a town and seeing a shrine to "the unknown god." Paul used that opportunity, recorded in the rest of the chapter, to tell them, "let me tell you something about that unknown God. I know Him, and He's the only true God that you should be believing in. All of the rest of them are false gods." It's a real blessing that God's Word is being given out to the country of India!

Remembering God's Word Shows Love

Next, keeping God's Word involves diligent studying of God's Word. Paul, in 2 Timothy 2:15, tells us, "Study to shew thyself approved unto God, a workman that needeth not to be ashamed." We know, however, that all the studying in the world is meaningless without God showing up and providing us with His revelation. It is God who reveals His truths, and God reveals His truths unto us as He sees fit. Perhaps most churches get an A+ for this, as well, because the teaching of God's Word is going on, and the studying of God's Word is happening.

Next, "keeping" involves learning and doing. You don't really keep God's Word until it actually becomes part of you, so ask yourself, how much time are you practicing this Holy vocation that God has given you? In the Word, it says, "what has hindered you?" or "what is distracting you?" We are also reminded to be not only hearers of God's Word but also doers of His word.

Keeping God's Word involves **diligent studying of God's Word.**

It is God who reveals His truths, and God reveals His truths unto us **as He sees fit.**

We all know that it's not faith, plus works equal Salvation. But if you have faith and you have Salvation, then you can be sure that God is going to perform some works through you. In this, the saints should get an A+ too, because we are active, and we are out here doing things and performing Christian works.

Notice how I clarified that thought, and instead of say-

Sermon 6 – Loving Christ and Keeping His Commandments

ing "the church," I said "the saints." I say this because not all church members are out there working for the Lord. What I'm talking about are those busy ones...the ones that are here on Wednesday night for prayer service and Bible study, and not the Sunday morning only.

Fourth and finally, Time magazine identified a man known as the most prevalent creature of the new Millennium. Who was it? It was Bishop T. D. Jakes! That's right. That is saying something in this day and age! This black man is the most powerful creature on the planet.

Now let's say you are sitting under his ministry, and you're thinking you have arrived. You are thinking, "I'm at the best church," "I have the best preacher," "I'm under the best ministry," and yet "I'm not really studying God's Word." You may think, "I'm going to the services" and "I'm listening to everything the Bishop is saying," but "I'm not really committing anything to memory."

Come Wednesday, am I really going to remember what he said on Sunday? Those of you who have a struggle remembering some facts, consider writing them down, and you may begin remembering more of them. If you refresh them in your mind, you may be surprised that you remember even more. I find that people tend to remember least what they value least. If they value something very highly, then they make a point to remember it.

Going back to what I said about falling in love, when you fall in love with somebody, you are going to commit to memory their favorite food, their favorite song, and their favorite color because you love them. You will do even more than that. You are going to commit to meeting their family. You're going to meet aunts, uncles, and cousins. And, over time, you are going to meet friends, neighbors, and classmates.

I find that people tend to remember least **what they value least.**

These are all people that have had at least some kind of small influence on your beloved. So, the value of remembering their names and how they are related to your beloved is now elevated. You have got to make sure that you remember that name or that relationship, and yet sometimes you don't.

But when your beloved mentions their name and you say "who it that," then your beloved will notice what you do and do not remember, and who you do and do not value. As you take the time to remember more and more about them, then they know that you love them because of that. You demonstrate your love for them by remembering that connection and remembering that relationship. Just like falling in love with your beloved is a love relationship, the same is true of the church falling in love with Christ.

Solomon, in Song of Solomon 2:8-10, recounts, "The

Sermon 6 – Loving Christ and Keeping His Commandments

voice of my beloved! behold, he cometh leaping upon the mountains, skipping upon the hills. My beloved is like a roe or a young hart: behold, he standeth behind our wall, he looketh forth at the windows, shewing himself through the lattice. My beloved spake, and said unto me, Rise up, my love, my fair one, and come away."

Later, Solomon, in Song of Solomon 4:1-2, describes his beloved saying, "behold, thou art fair; thou hast doves' eyes', within thy locks: thy hair is as a flock of goats, that appear from mount Gilead. Thy teeth are like a flock of sheep that are even shorn, which came up from the washing."

Further down at the end of that same chapter, in verse 16, Solomon recounts that his beloved replies, "Awake O north wind; and come, thou south; blow upon my garden, that the spices thereof may flow out. Let my beloved come into his garden and eat his pleasant fruits." This is the love a man has for a woman and a woman has for a man. If God made that love, then that makes it great. We all that are married have to remember that love. Because that's the love that Christ has for the church.

So, when I give you this, I'm giving you this straight from the Lord. How many of us are having a failing grade on this fourth one here? Divine wisdom is realizing something's worth learning is something worth doing. However, divine understanding is also realizing that some things are worth teaching and also some things worth remembering.

If we are not remembering God's Word enough, then perhaps we're not valuing the things of God. God's Word says that we are not to forget. In the Jewish synagogues back in the time of Jesus and even today, the Jewish men would wear a small box on their foreheads, which is called a phylactery. Inside the box would be scriptures, and several times a day, they would stop, open the box, and read the scripture to increase their spiritual memory.

> Some things are worth teaching and also some things worth remembering.

We must get to the point where we are studying and learning God's Word in new and more profound ways because it is only by getting God's Word in us that we truly grow spiritually. Do what you have to do to get God's Word in you.

We already talked about the importance of remembering, but what about teaching our next generation? Isn't that important too? Well, God tells us in Deuteronomy 6:7, "And thou shalt teach them diligently unto thy children, and shalt talk of them when thou sittest in thine house, and when thou walkest by the way, and when thou liest down, and when thou riseth up."

How much of God's Word are we learning ourselves, and how much of it are we teaching our children? How much time

Sermon 6 – Loving Christ and Keeping His Commandments

are we actually spending speaking God's Word and His promises? We need to go back to the old ways of whatever it takes to remember God's Word and His promises.

I'll end on this one truth from God. In Proverbs 4:7, it says, "Wisdom is the principal thing; therefore, get wisdom: and with all thy getting get understanding." Brothers and sister, we need to get wisdom, and we need to do our part to retain it. How can the Holy Spirit bring Holy scriptures to our remembrance if we have never taken the time to read them in the first place? Let us pray.

Lord, bless us, your children, and instill in us more of a desire to study Your Word and to want to know more about who You are. Help us make time to study Your Word regularly and to enjoy our time with You. For those of us who are responsible for young children, please encourage our hearts to teach the children in our homes and to be dedicated to bring them to Sunday school on time. Bless us, keep us, and help us have a renewed desire to learn at a deeper level of what thus sayeth the Lord! Now, let the church say amen and amen!

Sermon 7 – Partners in Christ's Suffering

Verses: 1 Peter 2:9-25
(Originally preached on September 2, 2007)

"But ye [are] a chosen generation, a royal priesthood, an holy nation, a peculiar people; that ye should shew forth the praises of Him who hath called you out of darkness into his marvelous light."

1 Peter 2:9-25

This morning's scripture comes to us from the book of 1 Peter, chapter 2, and verse 9. When you have found it in your Bibles, say "Amen!" Let us all stand to give honor to God's Word. Now that I don't hear any more pages turning, let me begin; and it says, "But ye are a chosen generation, a royal priesthood, an holy nation, a peculiar people; that ye should shew forth the praises of Him who hath called you out of darkness into his marvelous light; Which in time past were not a people, but are now the people of God: which had not obtained mercy, but now have obtained mercy.

Dearly beloved, I beseech you as strangers and pilgrims,

Sermon 7 – Partners in Christ's Suffering

abstain from fleshly lusts, which war against the soul; Having your conversation honest among the Gentiles: that, whereas they speak against you as evildoers, they may by your good works, which they shall behold, glorify God in the day of visitation. Submit yourselves to every ordinance of man for the Lord's sake: whether it be to the king, as supreme; Or unto governors, as unto them that are sent by him for the punishment of evildoers, and for the praise of them that do well.

For so is the will of God, that with well doing ye may put to silence the ignorance of foolish men: As free, and not using your liberty for a cloak of maliciousness, but as the servants of God. Honour all men. Love the brotherhood. Fear God. Honour the king. Servants be subject to your masters with all fear, not only to the good and gentle but also to the froward.

For this is thankworthy, if a man for conscience toward God endure grief, suffering wrongfully. For what glory is it if, when ye be buffeted for your faults, ye shall take it patiently? But if, when ye do well and suffer for it, ye take it patiently, this is acceptable with God. For even hereunto were ye called: because Christ also suffered for us, leaving us an example, that ye should follow his steps. Who did no sin, neither was guile found in his mouth: Who, when He was reviled, reviled not again; when He suffered, He threatened not; but committed Himself to Him that judgeth righteously: Who his own self bare our sins in His own body on the tree, that we, being dead to sins, should live unto righteousness: by whose stripes ye were healed. For ye were as sheep going astray but are now returned unto the Shepherd and Bishop of your souls."

Morning Prayer

Praise the Lord, church. Let us go right into prayer. Heavenly Father, we just thank You, Lord, for this beautiful day. We see the sun is shining, and there is not a cloud in the sky. Lord God, we thank You for waking us up this morning. You came by each one of our homes and woke us up, touched us with Your finger of love. Each one of us is here, and this is Your appointed time and Your appointed place for something spectacular to happen today.

We are counting on You, so Lord God, we ask You to come and reveal Yourself in Your Word that is being spoken today that the message and the understanding will be there. And that as a result, our lives will be changed for the better. Father God, don't let anyone walk out of here the way we walked in. Lord God, don't let anyone of us walk out of here with that form of darkness, not understanding why You do what it is You do.

> Each one of us is here, and this is **Your appointed time and Your appointed place** for something spectacular to happen today.

Sermon 7 – Partners in Christ's Suffering

We won't understand everything You do because You are God and we are not. But Lord God, You want us to understand Your ways, or You would not have written the Bible, which is our instruction manual. Lord God, we ask You to release in our mind an understanding in accordance to Your Word. Bless us, Lord God, and we will be blessed, in Jesus' mighty name, we pray, amen and amen!

> Bless us, Lord God, and **we will be blessed**, in Jesus' mighty name, we pray, amen and amen!

You were singing earlier this morning, and I could hear you guys rocking the place. I can hear that the people of God are on fire for the Lord. As I walked in, I heard you singing the Fred Hammond song, singing "I will dance like David danced," and "I will pray like David prayed." Let me ask you some questions: would you kill like David killed? Would you battle like David battled? Or would you slay a lion like David slayed a lion? Because that's what we are going to talk about today.

Our Children Suffering with Christ

We are going to talk about the suffering of Christ. It's not as glamorous a topic as maybe some other, but it's a needful topic. Because we are all going through something, Amen? Everyone is going through something. The adults may think, "My kids aren't suffering because if they need shoes, then I get them shoes." But, if you parents asked your kids, you might be surprised at the answer you get. The kids will tell you that they suffer in their comings and goings and at school, but mostly from their parents. How many kids would acknowledge that what I'm saying is right? Raise your hands.

> The kids will tell you that they suffer in their comings and goings and at school, **but mostly from their parents.**

How many of you feel like your parents are too tough on you and that your parents just don't understand you, and your parents don't agree with you when you are thinking of something. How many kids feel like they suffer? Children may say, "I need a cell phone because everyone else has a cell phone." If you have said that, kids, put your hands up high, come on. Kids, you have to realize that we adults come from a different generation than you.

We come with different experiences and different memories than you all do. Sure, you may be right, and all of the kids in your class all have cell phones, but we look back over our life thinking, "we never had a cell phone growing up, and we did just fine! We turned out all right. Whenever we wanted to see our friends, we just walked outside and played with them

Sermon 7 – Partners in Christ's Suffering

out there in the yard. Or, if they lived down the street, we just knocked on their door and said, let's go outside to play."

Our Suffering with Christ

So, it's a different generation, and it feels like a whole different world that we live in now. We have to understand that we all suffer differently, and we all have our own crosses to bear. I wish deacon Hickman was here because he preached a really good sermon not that long ago. He talked about "the Two Crosses of Christ." He said that there are two crosses that have to be carried. Christ bears the one, but we have to bear the other.

> There are two crosses that have to be carried. **Christ bears the one, but we have to bear the other.**

Don't think that there is just one cross, and that is that you get saved, and that's it. Don't think to yourself, "Go ahead, Jesus, you can carry all of my burdens now." We have got to suffer. Now that is not a pretty glamorous thing to say, but I'm going to bring it back around if you just have to hang in there with me.

We are going to have to suffer with Christ because if we suffer with Him, what happens? We are going to reign with

Him! Don't expect to reign and not suffer. As adults, we suffer, and just like we may not fully understand their suffering, the kids might not understand how we suffer. Sometimes we suffer on our jobs. Our children just see mom and dad whenever they come home from work, and yet they don't see all the suffering that goes on at their jobs.

There are some things you go through that you don't bring home to your daughters or your sons. You may be suffering in your body, and you don't want anyone to know. You try to put a smile on your face, but you are suffering inside, and other people just don't know all of the aching that's going on inside your body. We suffer in different ways, and we suffer at different times.

Sometimes that suffering can change. With the children, sometime during this school year, they may complain that they have to suffer under their teacher. How many kids can agree to that? Back in the early church, in the 1st century, there was a whole lot of suffering going on. Suffering is a kind of general thing. Suffering to you may not be suffering to me. Something that's hard on me may not be hard for the next person. But their suffering was unto death.

Examples of Christians Suffering

You have to understand that back then, there were those who actually thought that they were doing God a service if

Sermon 7 – Partners in Christ's Suffering

they killed you! If you were a Christian back then, the word "Christian" had the same connotation as today's word "terrorist." If I captured an active terrorist on the street today and announced, "Hey, I have captured a terrorist," people would celebrate me, and that's the way that they were treating Christians in the 1st century.

You think you have it rough now, but imagine what living life back then was like. Christians weren't getting mistreated only on one side, but they were getting mistreated on two sides. They were getting mistreated by the Jews, who felt that what they were doing was not the true religion. And they were getting it from the Romans, who used them as a political scapegoat. The Romans were so cruel to them that they would feed them to the bears and lions to be eaten in the Colosseum! They would put them in the big Colosseum and have them fight against trained gladiators.

Like we watch football today, the entertainment for the Romans back in that day was that they would force captured Christians in the Colosseum and then have the lions come out and tear them to pieces. So, it was rough back then. So, back in the 1st century, the desire of people to want to become a Christian and to go to a church and to get saved was starting to go down. But then there was the apostle Peter coming to encourage the early church, and he said to them, "You are going to go through some stuff!

But there is a reason for it. And there is a way to do it.

This summer, I had the opportunity to go on a missions trip to the country of Jamaica. I went to a place called the Iron Horse and to a boy's orphanage. It was a very sad place because what they had there were little boys like six-seventeen all mixed together.

Right then and there, anyone who has ever worked with kids would tell you; you don't put the little, little kids with the big kids. That all by itself set up a problem. But, then, on top of that, you had little kids that were there because they were abandoned. They haven't done anything wrong; it's just their parents felt that they couldn't keep them anymore. And then there were also intermixed in the group children who were criminals.

There was one boy that had stabbed someone, and that's why he had been sent there. So, you have this mixture of the innocent and the worst all mixed together. That is suffering. Similarly, their accommodations were terrible! I witnessed that they had several little boys held in what would be a little boy's prison cell. There were steel bars, and the young boys were crammed in there and sitting like birds sitting in a cage!

The good news, though, was that even there, we found that Jesus was being preached—hallelujah! While we were there, we met one boy named Carter. Inside the orphanage's compound, he had painted a mural from floor to ceiling and twenty-five feet long! He just used whatever paints he had there. The painting was of the apostle Peter getting out of the

Sermon 7 – Partners in Christ's Suffering

boat to join Jesus walking on the water.

Where does that come from? God oftentimes sends these glimmers of hope and light into the darkest of our situations. There was another situation where three little boys came up to me and said, "just read the Word." That's all they wanted. They didn't want money, candy, or soda. They said, "read from the Bible" because they hadn't heard the Bible. So, suffering can take on different meanings.

I kind of think back on verse 9, which says that we are a "chosen generation." A chosen generation makes you stick your chest out and feel confident. How many of us can remember back when we were kids that when it came time for picking teams, you didn't want to be the last one picked? Or worse, you didn't want to be the one not picked at all! Can you remember those days? And then verses 9 and 10 say you are a royal priesthood. That makes you want to poke your chest out, saying, "yeah, that's my Heavenly Daddy."

> you are a royal priesthood. That makes you want to poke your chest out, saying, "yeah, that's my Heavenly Daddy.

It's at a time like that that you think to yourself that that's my Heavenly Daddy who owns everything…yeah, that's my Daddy. It says that you are a part of a holy nation. Holy means "for use by God." That's what makes the Bible Holy; it's be-

God's Purpose and Plan for your Life

cause it is "for us by God." In the same way, you are Holy because you are for God's use, too, if you let Him. That's right, poke your chest out and pat yourself on the back because you are for use by God.

You are as Holy as the Bible. Who said it, the Bible! But now the scriptures start to get a little different and says that you are a peculiar people. You could be at home cutting your grass right now or washing your car right now, but instead, you are up here in church. Y'all are peculiar.

What we Might Consider Suffering

Some of you got up at 7 a.m. this Sunday morning to prepare yourself and your family for church today, and some of you got up at 6 a.m. to be here today. Something is wrong with y'all because you are peculiar. Some of y'all gave $50 to the church, some gave $100, and some gave $100 when you could have saved that money and bought yourself something nice with that money. Y'all are peculiar.

Back when you were in the world, if someone called you peculiar, you might not have liked it, and those would have become fighting words! But, now that you have been saved and born again, you realize that there isn't anything wrong with you and proving to yourself that there has been a change in you—you're a new man or woman of God.

Your new man doesn't have a problem with being peculiar,

Sermon 7 – Partners in Christ's Suffering

and you don't have a problem with being Holy, royal, or being chosen. Because you see, there is a difference between what happens here on earth and what happens in heaven. You're already starting to change. You've already started taking your eyes off humanity and put your eyes on divinity and seeing your future world.

Still, there are different types of suffering. You can suffer by having some affliction in you, but you can also suffer by giving up something that you really want. Like during the time of Lent, people would say that they are not going to eat chocolate for forty days so that it will show Christ that they really value what He did. That isn't really a sacrifice, though, is it? How about give up food for forty days and see how you do then.

Jesus did it! Didn't He go out in the desert for forty days and forty nights? If we want to truly suffer for Christ, perhaps we should try giving up something that is really going to hurt, and that is really going to hit us in the seat of our emotions. I think the young women and young men that are right now serving our country in war are suffering. They are far from home, they don't have access to their families, and they are paying with the most valuable thing that they have…their lives.

On top of that, they are fighting a war that is a different kind of war than what it was back in World War II, Korea, and even Vietnam. Today, they may have some jobs where all they do is stand a post, but they have to constantly be diligent because, at any moment, their world could be overdue to

God's Purpose and Plan for your Life

truck bombings and anti-personnel rockets.

We have to realize that there is real suffering going on today, which can help all of us put our suffering in context. Verse 12 says, "Having your conversation honest among the gentiles." How many of us suffer from our conversation? How many times have we said things that later we thought that we shouldn't have said? We have to realize that we are being watched by the world and that someday soon, we will be held accountable. You are held accountable for every single word that comes out of your mouth. Think about that!

The scripture continues by saying, "Dearly beloved, I beseech you as strangers and pilgrim," so you are not really from here. Peter is not talking to the earthly Darnell from Manassas, but instead, he is talking to the new creature Brother Darnell from heaven.

Peter goes on saying, "abstain, run from, and avoid fleshly lust." Some of you may think that you don't do that, and you may feel that you are cool with that part of the Bible because it doesn't affect you. But this is about us because we are all in this together.

Philippians 2:5 says, "Let this mind be in you which was also in Christ Jesus." Why am I bringing up the mind when discussing a scripture regarding fleshly lust? Are you starting to get where I'm going? Maybe not. Think about this; it has been said, "mind your attitude because your attitude will de-

Sermon 7 – Partners in Christ's Suffering

termine what you will and will not think about."

It starts way back in your mind in the form of your attitude. How many times do we parents look at our children and check them on their attitudes? But where do we think the children are getting these negative attitudes from? And, who do we think the children are looking at? Touch your neighbor and tell them, "children will only do what they see!" They will mimic what they are around.

*Be careful with your thoughts because they will **determine the words that come out of your mouth.***

Now I won't put it all on the parents because there are other things that children watch and see. They are watching TV, they go to the movies, and they are listening to the radio. Just like with our own children, start with the attitude, and that will control what we think about.

Before we let those words come out of our mouths, ask ourselves, **is it kind, is it needful, and is it true?**

Be careful with your thoughts because they will determine the words that come out of your mouth. Have you ever said something without fully thinking it out first? Do you find that you often talk without

154

thinking? Do you routinely find yourself saying, "Oh, I didn't mean to say that?"

But, wait! What does that mean? Your own brain thought out the words, and then your own mouth said it. Pastor has always taught us for years that before we speak anything to anyone, to first run it through three tests. Before we let those words come out of our mouths, ask ourselves, is it kind, is it needful, and is it true?

We may all know people who only check for one thing, is it true, and if it passes as true, then out it comes out of their mouth. We tend to describe people like that as having no filter. So, let us all check ourselves because before speaking, we all really need to work on checking that our words are both kind and needful.

I had a situation with one of my daughters when I was attending a sporting event in which my other daughter was performing. I had to put our family's video camera on its tripod, put a videotape in it, and turned the camera on. I walked away, yet not only did it captured the sporting event, but it also captured all of the things going on along the sidelines, as well. Later on, after the sporting event was over, we all went home, and I didn't watch the video for a while.

However, when I finally did watch the video, I was absolutely appalled at my own behavior on the sidelines! I was only into the first five minutes of the videotape, and you couldn't

Sermon 7 – Partners in Christ's Suffering

imagine how rough I was being on my daughter. On the videotape, I could hear someone yelling at her and thought to myself, "who is this yelling at my daughter?" But it was me! Had I not videotaped it and saw with my own eyes how my daughters see me and how their friends see me…I never would have believed it!

We sit up here in this church and sing that song "if I looked at myself through God's eyes, what would I see." But what about if I looked at myself through my children's eyes? What would I see? We teach them to obey the rules and obey the laws, and yet we are speeding. They see the sign that says "no turn on red," while they also see their parents thinking, "because I have places to go and nobody's around," and then they turn anyway.

Police officers have no patience for people who are in a rush because they know that you are speeding because of a lack of planning. They believe that if you hadn't chosen to leave late, there would be no need for speeding. Or, if you had chosen to leave early, you would have taken your time, and you wouldn't be in a rush.

There is no reason to speed in the eyes of a police officer. Now, if he pulls you over and s/he finds out that the reason you are speeding is because your passenger has had an accident, is bleeding, and you are trying to rush them to the hospital, then they might not write you a ticket because that's a reasonable excuse. But all other excuses, like "I'm late" or

"I have to get to work," are your problem.

Poor planning equals tickets. When little children sit in the back seats, their eyes are perfectly aligned with the street signs and your speedometer. They can see how fast you are going. And then you get out of the car and tell them don't do this, don't do that, and don't cross the street on a red light, but then why should we think that they are going to listen to us? Children might think, "You spoke one thing to us but acted another way." They hear our words, and they see our actions; now, which one do you think they are actually going to follow? Children will actually first do what you do, and then second do what you say do.

So, your thoughts control your words. If you don't keep check of your words, pretty soon, they turn into your actions. You ever hear a person say, "Man, if you keep messing with me, I'm going to bust you up?" And then, pretty soon, you see the person bust him up because the other person just kept on speaking

Children will actually first **do what you do**, and then second **do what you say do.**

If you are not careful, you may be speaking words into existence that are **slowly cutting away at your life.**

Sermon 7 – Partners in Christ's Suffering

those words into existence.

A lot of times, we need to put our mouths in check. A lot of times, you are speaking things into existence that you don't realize. Not always toward someone else, but oftentimes even towards yourself. What about when you are driving in traffic, and someone cuts you off, and you say, "Man, you're killing me?" What you really mean is "your driving is stressing me out," but that's not what you said, is it? Do you know what you just said?

If you are not careful, you may be speaking words into existence that are slowly cutting away at your life. So, let's be careful about what we speak because words do become actions. And, if you do the same actions long enough, then it becomes a habit. And, if you do a habit long enough, then it becomes part of your character. Do you know what a habit is? A habit is something you can't stop when you are ready to. So, the habit now takes control of you.

If you allow it to get into your character, it will form your future destiny. Do you have a habit of smoking cigarettes your whole life? Then, there may be a destiny that involves lung cancer, throat cancer, and mouth cancer. Do you have a habit of a lustful mind and you want to be into sexual, dirty things, then let it run to completion, and let's see what that can get you, including out-of-wedlock pregnancies, STDs, and diseases that can take you out of here! There's a price to pay for not keeping check on these things. So, we want to be able to put a guard over our mouths and avoid lustful things.

Verse 12 tells us, "Having your conversation honest among the Gentiles: that, whereas they speak against you as evildoers, they may by your good works, which they shall behold, glorify God in the day of visitation." You may ask the question "why do I have to suffer to go through things?" and "why do I have to mind things that other people do not have to mind?"

Well, go back to verse 10, which reads, "which had not obtained mercy, but now have obtained mercy." There is a cost. There is a cost for your salvation and mercy. That's a life of suffering. It's the suffering that leads us to do what needs to be done for the furthering of God's Kingdom.

Sometimes you don't feel like coming to church, so that might be your suffering, thinking to yourself, "I have to suffer to make it one more week!" Be careful what you say now because what you are talking about now are the things we do in the church. A lot of us are leaders in the church, and I know for a fact that the leaders here don't suffer to do their ministry and their different functions in the church; but instead, they count it a joy to serve the Lord and the chil-

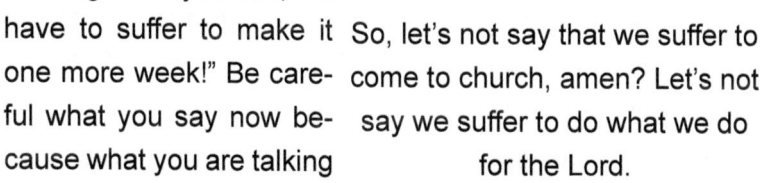

> So, let's not say that we suffer to come to church, amen? Let's not say we suffer to do what we do for the Lord.

Sermon 7 – Partners in Christ's Suffering

dren of God!

You think the choir sings good on Sunday; then you should come by here on a Thursday night during choir rehearsal! That's all I'm going to say about our lovely choir. If you are here in church, you get two songs. But on Thursday night, they will sing nine, ten, or eleven songs! So, let's not say that we suffer to come to church, amen? Let's not say we suffer to do what we do for the Lord.

For those who aren't in leadership yet and maybe want a position in the church, do you really understand what you are asking? Be careful what you ask for. What you ask for and what you get might not be the same thing. You want to be in leadership, but leadership comes with a cost.

A new pastor comes to a new town. He gets on the bus in a new town where he is pastoring this new church and pays the fare. The bus driver gives him the wrong change, but he doesn't realize it though. He finds his seat and counts the change, but quickly realizes that the change was off, in that the bus driver gave him too much money back.

So, during the ride, he contemplated if he should give the money back or shouldn't he. He runs through all the scriptures in the Bible that say "do unto others as you would want them to do unto you" and "thou shall not steal." But then he had these other scriptures competing with them.

In the end, he thought, "should I bother this man while

he's working since it's only 25¢?" At the end of the trip, he gets up and decides he's not going to debate this with himself any longer, and he gives the bus driver the 25¢ as he was getting off. The bus driver stops him and says, "Sir, I recognized you as the new pastor in town, and this was a test. I purposely gave you that extra quarter because my wife and I are looking for a new church, and we wanted to know if we were coming to your church. You passed the test, so you'll see us there Sunday!"

*If the devil tries to remind you of your past, **rebuke him and remind him of his future!***

Do you realize that the world is watching you? We have about seven people getting baptized today. New converts, do understand that when you get baptized, all of your friends are going to look at you differently. You are making a statement that "you are no longer that person you were yesterday," that "you have Christ inside of you and you are a new creature," and that "the past is put away." If the devil tries to remind you of your past, rebuke him and remind him of his future!

Sometimes we have to suffer for living right. Now, that sounds like a conflict, but it isn't. Sometimes you think to do as your neighbor does, and you are tempted to think, "They don't do right, so then I don't have to do right either." But is that really the right thing to do? We are to suffer with Christ, if

Sermon 7 – Partners in Christ's Suffering

we are going to reign with Him. It's not "suffer through Him," it's "suffer with Him." That means as He suffered, so shall we suffer.

Verse 13 says, "Submit yourselves to every ordinance of man for the Lord's sake: whether it be to the king, as supreme." How many of us have said something negative out of our mouths about President Bush? Let's be honest. I see little kids putting their hands up. What does that tell you? God is saying to you, don't do that. I'm going to pull it all together at the end of this message, but don't do that any longer. When you say something negative against the leader, you are saying something negative against the One who put Him in position.

In the Bible, it says, when I fault you, I'm not faulting you; I'm faulting the creator who created you. Don't do these negative things to other children of God because it's passing through that person and going directly to God. You might think that God didn't put President George Bush into the position, but He allowed it. In Psalm 75:6-7, God warns us, "For promotion cometh neither from the east, nor from the west, nor from the south. But God is the judge: He putteth down one, and setteth up another." We have to be mindful of that, and we have to act accordingly.

In 1 Peter 2:14, it continues saying, "Or unto governors, as unto them that are sent by him for the punishment of evildoers, and for the praise of them that do well. For so is the will of

God, that with well doing ye may put to silence the ignorance of foolish men." When you hear the Bible use the word "foolish" or "fool," is it speaking of someone who doesn't believe in God. Again, all the eyes of the world are on you. They are on you when you get baptized, and they are on us now. And, I don't care how long you've been saved; they are still on you!

You could have been saved twenty years, and still, I guarantee you that there's someone on your job watching you. They are watching for every little mistake. And they love to say things like, "See, I thought you were a Christian!" Where is it that they all use the same sentence? They didn't say anything for the 364 days this year, all while you were doing well. But then, that one day you mess up, there they are to catch you. That's because their eyes are always on you. I remember brother Rob preached a message about "The Battle is On!" He was reminding us and actually informing some of us that we are in the midst of a war.

You can get saved, you can be going to church and thinking everything is cool, but not really realizing that there is a battle going on for ever-loving your soul and for the souls of your children. If you are not prepared, and you think everything is fine and it's not, then you are about ready to get taken out of here. In his sermon, he preached about the importance of putting on the whole armor of God and being prepared and not going out into this world unprepared. We need to get ourselves geared up and silence the ignorance of foolish men.

Sermon 7 – Partners in Christ's Suffering

In verses 16-17, it says, "As free, and not using your liberty for a cloke of maliciousness, but as the servants of God. Honour all men. Love the brotherhood. Fear God. Honour the king." Well, in 1 Corinthians 6:12 and then again in 1 Corinthians 10:23, it says, "all things are lawful for me but not all things are expedient for me."

You have to realize that you have a freedom that others don't have, but you shouldn't use that freedom to hurt people. I was telling you earlier that a lot of people will speak things that are not needful or kind. They will just say it, but that is not scriptural because here, the scripture tells us to edify and build up one another and not go through and tear down one another.

> And if you're not doing anything righteously in God's eyes, then it's as if **you aren't doing it at all.**

We have to suffer to do good. Your good does not matter to God if it's not done for the right reasons. It doesn't matter to God that you go and give $1,000 to the church if you didn't do it cheerfully or with the right motives. His Word talks about righteousness, which is right thinking, right living, and rightness. And if you're not doing anything righteously in God's eyes, then it's as if you aren't doing it at all. It says it's better for you to keep your money than to give wrongly. You are supposed to pay your tithes and to give your offerings cheerfully because God loves a cheerful giver.

Using that same structure, you might say that I asked God to be a leader within the church, and instead, God taught me to be a follower because you'll never respect being a leader unless you first learn how to follow someone. On one of his teaching videotapes, it was Dr. John Maxwell that said, "If you are a leader and no one is following you, then you are just a person out on a walk."

Similarly, someone may ask God for help so that they may do greater things, but instead, He allowed them infirmity that through Him, they can do things greater. Oftentimes we want perfect help, and we want our suffering to end. That's what we are praying to God at night about, but He may be saying, "I allowed that suffering to be only for a while." While you are in the midst of that infirmity, are you still going to praise Him, and is He still going to be able to work through you to do greater things in the midst of your suffering?

When it's all over, and your suffering has been lifted, will you be able to look back over those years and say, "look what I've accomplished," or "look what God has accomplished through me" ? I've learned to let go and allowed God to handle it.

Christians Suffering in Perspective

Ask God for riches so that you might be happy, and instead, He may give you poverty that you will become truly

Sermon 7 – Partners in Christ's Suffering

thankful for all He has already provided you. Thinking about my recent missions trip to Jamaica, I tell you what. If I could take each and every one of you with me next time, I would.

You would be surprised how little some people have whenever you travel to some of these countries, and yet they don't seem sad about it. When I was over there, their small shacks and houses had nothing in them…no furniture! Some of them were only one room, and that was the whole house. In the morning, that room is the kitchen, in the afternoon that same room became the living room, and at night that room became the bedroom, yet every single one of these shacks and small houses had a TV in it!

If you have a TV, then you know what's available out there in the world. You know that people have cars, clothes, and food, and you know people have good stuff. So, if they have very little and they are alright with it, how bad are we? We may think we are poor, yet we have got money in the bank. Each one of us rode up here in something with four wheels. I didn't see anyone riding a bike here. Am I saying it right? We have to really keep ourselves in check.

If you get up in the middle of the night and you want a glass of water, then you go to the sink, and you turn the faucet, and outcomes cold water or hot water. Don't you understand that in Jamaica, in the morning, they send the kids about five to ten blocks down the road to a communal tap. Then, these poor children have to carry these five-gallon buckets full of water

God's Purpose and Plan for your Life

all the way back home, every day! Out of that water, they use it to brush their teeth, wash their body, cook, and clean. You walk to the bathroom, and your water is there, clean, hot, and warm, and delivered right to you.

Now, even though we have water that comes to us directly, we still go out and buy water in a plastic bottle with a label on it. What's next, a bottle of water that you don't even have to unscrew the top off of, and instead, you just speak to it, and it opens up? Brothers and sisters, what more do we really want from God?

We might ask God for power so that we can have the praise of men, and instead, God may give us weakness that we might feel our need for God. How many of us own our own businesses? Okay, only a few of us. How many of the rest of us work for somebody? Those that own your own business, since you don't really work for anybody else, you can think of it as you work for your clients and your customers since everybody answers to somebody.

A lot of times we suffer on our jobs. You get up some days thinking, "Why do I have to go to work today?" I heard it said on the radio last week that they surveyed a group of people on how many people dread getting up in the morning having to go to their jobs. In this city, the number was 64 percent! That means two out of every three people dread getting up in the morning to go to work! In this city, that means that there is only one person in three that gets up in the morning happy

Sermon 7 – Partners in Christ's Suffering

and ready to go to work.

That means that many of us feel that just going to work involves something that we will have to suffer through. It could be a boss that doesn't understand you and is there just to give you a hard time. Or, it could be that the job you do is a very hard job to do.

Verse 18 says, "Servants, in reverent fear of God submit yourselves to your masters, not only to those who are good and considerate, but also to those who are harsh." Again, if you go through life and you are not suffering for nothing, then don't expect to reign. If you have a boss that is not the perfect boss, welcome to the party! Everyone is carrying some burden.

The scripture continues, "For this is thankworthy, if a man for conscience toward God endure grief, suffering wrongfully." If tonight you feel like you are suffering on your job, then I would get this scripture blown up and put it on your desk or somewhere where you feel that your suffering is going on. God says that what you are doing is worth Him thanking you. How many times has God thanked you for anything…and how many times has He come out of heaven and said, "thank you for doing that?" Do you want God's thanks? Well, here it is right here.

If you suffer because you messed up, that doesn't count. God is not going to thank you for that. If you messed up, then sometimes you have to pay that price. But if you are suffering wrongfully, like someone is scandalizing your name, then God is thanking you. Stand still and receive your thanks from God.

It says," For what glory is it, if when ye be buffeted for your faults." How many times have we done something, and we were like, "What were we thinking doing that?" How many times have we done that, and we say to ourselves, "I hope no one else knows?"

Recently on the news, it was reported that there was a senator that got caught in an airport bathroom doing something he wasn't supposed to, and now he's been removed from office. He thought what he did was not going to be seen by anyone, but the devil always makes sure there is someone there to see it and report it. I'm going to tell you, don't go out hereafter today and think you can do something and it will not be seen, because as I said, the world is watching you…and the devil is watching you too! So be careful what you say because he's recording everything you say too. The devil watches you and looks for those little weaknesses.

I don't know about you, but I want all of my works to be **received by God.**

So what glory is it if you are getting beat up for your own fault? He says if you are getting treated like that, then you

Sermon 7 – *Partners in Christ's Suffering*

should take it patiently. But if you are out here doing well, and you still have to suffer for it, and you do it with patience, this is acceptable or received by God. I don't know about you, but I want all of my works to be received by God. I would hate to be doing all this work down here on earth, and then when we get to heaven, God says that it was not acceptable. If I'm going to suffer, I want to suffer and get God's reward for it.

We talked about having bad bosses, but sometimes it's not the boss that's the problem...it's your coworker. Maybe that is God's assignment for you. You're trying to work with this individual, but you feel like they have a manual for where all of your buttons are because they're pushing them all. Every time you try to turn the other cheek and say a scripture, they can find the next button, start pushing it, and BAMMM! You say to yourself, "Lord, are you sure this one is supposed to be saved?" You have to realize that this is a form of suffering too. But be patient through it because it is acceptable to God.

There's a book called Dealing with Difficult People written by a guy named Roy Lilley. He says, "think about it, you can choose your friends, what neighborhood you live in, how you spend your money, how you choose your mate, and you can even choose your job. But there are two things you can't choose, which are your family and your coworkers!" You have to realize that's a form of suffering too. Christ was our example, and He suffered long.

The last two scriptures, verses 24 and 25, are for those

God's Purpose and Plan for your Life

people who are suffering from health issues because they can be a cyclical thing. You start to get better, then it gets worse, then it starts getting better, and you think you are getting ahead, and then again, you are two steps back! It reads, "Who his own self bare our sins in His own body on the tree, that we, being dead to sins, should live unto righteousness: by whose stripes ye were healed." That right there should tell you that all healing comes from Christ. There is a power in illness, but there is a greater, more powerful power in Jesus Christ!

You have Jesus Christ in you, but have you unlocked the power of Christ in you for your health? A lot of times, people will struggle with something, not realizing that the answer is right there at their fingertips. You have to let it go and let the Lord take control of your health.

Some people battle with telling the truth on a regular basis, yet that's not an issue with salvation because you can be saved and still have a problem with lying. If you give it over to the Lord, He will correct that in you. I'm a witness to that. Just like in health situations, not everyone needs to run to the doctor. Doctors are now finding that oftentimes people with cancer had something called dormant cancer.

If you left it alone, it would leave you alone. But if you start to mess with it, it stimulates something throughout your body, and then all of a sudden, all of these cancers start popping up in your body! The bottom line is suffering in the areas of health, job, or money is all a part of your important walk with

Sermon 7 – Partners in Christ's Suffering

the Lord. First Peter 4:13-16, "But rejoice, inasmuch as ye are partakers of Christ's sufferings; that, when his glory shall be revealed, ye may be glad also with exceeding joy.

If ye be reproached for the name of Christ, happy are ye; for the spirit of glory and of God resteth upon you: on their part, He is evil spoken of, but on your part, He is glorified. But let none of you suffer as a murderer, or as a thief, or as an evildoer, or as a busybody in other men's matters. Yet if any man suffers as a Christian, let him not be ashamed; but let him glorify God on this behalf."

So, what is the reason for your suffering? To glorify God. We may sit here in church and say, "glory be to God," but do we really know what we mean when we say that? Yes, if we are going to reign with Christ, then first we have to suffer with Christ.

You are going to find that you're suffering in these certain areas in your life, but have faith because in time, you will reign! These very things you are asking the Lord for, they are coming—praise God! They are tied with your letting go of you. The reason why some of you may not want to suffer is because you still have a hand on the old man, but be encouraged and keep in mind that we are to suffer with Christ, and then we reign with Christ—hallelujah!

Apendix A – Sermon Scripture References

Sermon 1—2 Thessalonians 1:1-12 (KJV); Jeremiah 3:15 (KJV); Genesis 3:15 (KJV); 1 Corinthians 2:9 (KJV); and 1 Peter 5:10 (KJV).

Sermon 2—Genesis 4:1-7 (KJV); 2 Chronicles 25 (KJV); Philippians 2:5 (KJV); Isaiah 29:13 (KJV); Matthew 15:8 (KJV); Mark 7:6 (KJV); Luke 18:9-14 (KJV); James 4:7-8 (KJV); and Jude 1:11 (KJV).

Sermon 3—Ephesians: 3:16-19 (KJV); Malachi 3:6 (KJV); Romans 8:38-39 (KJV); Philippians 3:4-8 (KJV); Philippians 4:8 (KJV); Matthew 21:21 (KJV); Mark 11:23 (KJV); and Ephesians 4:26 (KJV).

Apendix A – Sermon Scripture References

Sermon 4—John 16:7-16 (KJV); John 14:16-18 (KJV); Romans 5:8 (KJV); Genesis 1: 26 (KJV); Genesis 11:7 (KJV); 1 John 5:7 (KJV); Matthew 3:16-17 (KJV); John 16:3 (KJV); Matthew 5:20 (KJV); Acts 5:1-10 (KJV); Ephesians 4:29-32 (KJV); 1 Corinthians 15:33 (KJV); and 1 Thessalonians 5:19 (KJV).

Sermon 5—1 Corinthians 5:17 (KJV); Ephesians 2:3 (KJV); Philippians 2:5 (KJV); Luke 23:34 (KJV); John 8:11 (KJV); 1 Peter 1:13 (KJV); Romans 12:1-2 (KJV); Romans 10:10 (KJV); Hebrews 3:8 (KJV); Ecclesiastes 4:12 (KJV); Romans 10: 8-10 (KJV); Psalm 103:12 (KJV); 1 Corinthians 12:13 (KJV); and Romans 6:4 (KJV).

Sermon 6—John 14:15 (KJV); Proverbs 7:1-3 (KJV); Proverbs 3:3 (KJV); Romans 10:14 (KJV); Acts 17:23 (KJV); Song of Solomon 2:8-10 (KJV); Song of Solomon 4:1-2 (KJV); Song of Solomon 4:16 (KJV); and Deuteronomy 6:7 (KJV).

Sermon 7—1 Peter 2:9-25 (KJV); Philippians 2:5 (KJV); Psalm 75:6-7 (KJV); 1 Corinthians 6:12 (KJV); 1 Corinthians 10:23 (KJV); and 1 Peter 4:13-16 (KJV).

God's Purpose and Plan for your Life

ADDITIONAL RESOURCES

Sermon Outline Template

Title: " "	Date: Sunday, AM Service
Verses:	
Opening Prayer:	
Notes:	
•	
•	
•	
•	
•	
Closing Prayer:	

Additional Online Resources

Just like when we get mail from a loved one, we don't say that the message was from the postman or woman who delivered our mail. Similarly, when preparing a sermon, we must first remember that the sermon is not ours. Instead, it is the Lord's. We are simply the messenger. Even our ministry is not our own, but it came from the Lord.

Next, you may be tempted to preach on something faddish or a topic given to you by another, but if the Lord doesn't tell you to preach those words, don't preach them. Preach only what the Lord lays on your heart to preach. First and foremost, you are God's messenger. Study God's Word closely and pray to Him, then He will lead you to what to preach.

Don't start your sermon preparations by reading a series of Bible commentaries looking at the godly revelation given to other pastors. Instead, prayerfully do your search believing in faith that if you seek, you will find because God will never let you down. On the following pages are a few free online tools that I have found useful in my sermon preparations that may be of assistance to you:

Additional Online Resources

Bible Gateway — This is a website designed to provide you with easy studying and searching of the Bible in various versions (like KJV, NIV, and ASB) and translations (like English, French, and Spanish). The website is free to use but also offers a membership program with enhanced services.

    Located at: http://www.BibleGateway.com.

Daily Bible Reading — The American Bible Society seeks to grow and improved Christians in scriptural knowledge using their Daily Bible Reading Guide. A copy of the current year's Bible Reading Guide can be downloaded from their site and printed. Readings for each month and year are based upon religious themes.

    Located at: https://www.americanbible.org/resources/daily-bible-reading.

Merriam-Webster Dictionary — This is the online version of the Merriam-Webster dictionary that also provides a diverse array of print and digital language references materials, including Merriam-Webster's Collegiate® Dictionary and the online Merriam-Webster Unabridged.

    Located at: https://www.merriam-webster.com/.

An additional online Bible-specific dictionary includes the **Easton's Bible Dictionary** located at: https://www.Biblegateway.com/resources/eastons-Bible-dictionary/Heading-A.

Hardbound and paperback editions of other popular Bible dictionaries at cost are: **The New Unger's Bible Dictionary** (by Moody Publishing), **Vine's Complete Expository Dictionary of Old and New Testament Words** (by HarperCollins Christian Publishing), and **Nelson's Illustrated Bible Dictionary: New and Enhanced Edition.**

Hitchcock's Bible Names — This online dictionary contains more than 2,500 Bible and Bible-related proper names and their meanings.

Located at: https://www.Biblegateway.com/resources/hitchcocks-Bible-names-dictionary/Heading-A.

Three additional online descriptions of Bible names include the **Smith's Bible Names Dictionary** located at:

https://www.Biblegateway.com/resources/smiths-Bi-

Additional Online Resources

ble-names-dictionary/Heading-A, **All the Men of the Bible** located at:

https://www.Biblegateway.com/resources/all-men-Bible/Romantic-History-Bible-Names and, **All the Women of the Bible** located at:

https://www.Biblegateway.com/resources/all-women-Bible/Introduction.

Macmillan Bible Atlas — This online atlas is a book on the geography, civilizations and cartography of the Holy Land. It describes the movements of biblical characters, trade routes and battles. It also refers to archaeological excavations, illustrations of artifacts, and a comparative chronology of early civilizations that relate to the Bible.

Located at: https://Bibleatlas.org/.

Hardbound and paperback editions of other popular Bible atlases at cost are: **The New Moody Atlas of the Bible**, **The Historical Atlas of the Bible Lands** (by Penguin Publishing), and **The Oxford Bible Atlas** (by Oxford University Press).

Dictionary of Bible Themes —This online resource is an easy-to-use dictionary of Bible themes.

Located at: https://www.Biblegateway.com/resources/dictionary-of-Bible-themes/toc.

Encyclopedia of the Bible —This online encyclopedia is derived from The Zondervan Pictorial Encyclopedia of the Bible, 5 Volume Set.

Located at: https://www.Biblegateway.com/resources/encyclopedia-of-the-Bible/toc.

Thru the Bible — As part of the ministry of Dr. J.Vernon McGee, in-depth notes are provided for 66 books of the Bible. These notes are free of charge and can be downloaded in .PDF format.

Located at: https://ttb.org/resources/notes-outlines-downloads.

Please note that these URL links were active on the date of the writing of this book. There is no guarantee they will still be active over time. If the links do not work, try typing the name of the online resource into your search engine of choice, such as Google.com.